OFFICE LOCATION AND THE JOURNEY TO WORK

For
Carole, Paul and Charlotte

Office Location and The Journey to Work

A Comparative Study of Five Urban Areas

Peter Walters

P. W. DANIELS
University of Liverpool

Gower
and
Retailing and Planning Associates

© P.W. Daniels 1980

Published by
Gower Publishing Company Limited,
Westmead, Farnborough, Hants, England, and
Retailing and Planning Associates,
P.O. Box 5, Corbridge, Northumberland.

Daniels, Peter Watters
   Office location and the journey to work.
   1. Commuting - England - Case studies
   2. Offices - Location - England - Case studies
   I. Title II. Retailing and Planning Associates
   388.4   HE244

   ISBN 0-566-00352-X

Printed in Great Britain by David Green (Printers) Limited
Kettering, Northamptonshire.

iv

Contents

Tables

Figures

Preface

This monograph presents some of the results from a
research project sponsored by the Department of the
Environment between September 1975 and March 1979.
The Location of Offices Bureau also provided some
assistance to cover the cost of questionnaire processing.
The Office Decentralization Project was divided into
two parts: the first part was a follow-up study of
the journey to work of office workers in decentralized
offices located in a wide range of centres throughout
Britain. This was designed to re-examine some · of
the conclusions of an earlier study first reported
in detail in 1972. The second part of the Project,
which forms the basis for the research reported here,
was largely concerned with a comparison of the journey
to work and residential location behaviour of employees
in several decentralized offices grouped in five urban
areas of varying size and location. The interpretation
of the survey data is purely my own and not necessarily
that of the Department of the Environment. Much of
the text and all the charts and tables are Crown Copyright
and I am grateful to the Head of Economics, Urban
and Regional Division of the Department of the Environment
for permission to use the material. The publication
of the manuscript would have been impossible without
the generous financial assistance provided by the
Department of Geography and the University of Liverpool.

The progress of this Project has depended at various
times on the co-operation of a large number of individuals
and organisations; those employed as part of the research
team, colleagues in the Geography Department and in
other Departments of the University of Liverpool,
and the organisations who allowed their employees
valuable time to participate in the Project. I am
indebted in particular to the Project's Research Assistant
Mr. A.W. Duffett, for accepting the responsibility
for managing the substantial task of data collection
and the subsequent task of processing and analysis
with enthusiasm and skill. Without his computing
skills and the techniques of data capture and data
handling which he researched and implemented to accommo-
date the large data set generated by both surveys,
the task of putting this book together would have
been impossible. The Project also relied on two part-
time secretaries, during its existence and the variety
of work involved has been completed with great speed,
accuracy and diligence, and not without humour, by
Mrs. Joan Stevenson and Mrs. Pauline Hobson. The
latter worked for a short period at the start of the
Project.

A great deal of assistance has also been received from members of staff in the Department of Geography. Cartographic work for the report has been undertaken by Miss Joan Treasure of the Department's Cartographic Unit. Miss Pauline Round, Map Curator in the Department of Geography, also provided valuable guidance and assistance with the assembly of diverse street plans and Ordnance Survey maps required for the purpose of processing the addresses given in the questionnaires. The Photographic Unit of the Faculty of Social and Environmental Studies assisted with the reduction of cartographic work into a form suitable for reproduction. Particular thanks are also due to Professor R. Lawton, Head of the Department of Geography, for providing spacious accommodation for the Project staff and for allowing the Department's Map Room to be used for accommodating temporary research assistants during the summer vacations in 1976 and 1977.

The scale of data processing and analysis for this Project has also required frequent contact for advice and assistance with other departments in this University, not least the Computer Centre and its staff. They have provided frequent assistance with problems ranging from methods of data capture through to the resolution of problems arising from the application of package programmes such as SYMAP and SPSS5 to the survey data. Particular thanks are due to Mr. A.D. Goddard, Mrs. B.J. Lowndes and Mr. K. Sharman (Computer Manager). Mrs. P. Hogan and her more recent successor handled without loss a very large number of OPSCAN forms upon which the raw data was recorded and the associated paper tape output. Data processing was also greatly assisted by a group of temporary research assistants who were employed in the summer of 1976 and 1977 to code and transfer the questionnaire information to the OPSCAN forms. Messrs. Bartlett, Rummery and Crabb; the Misses Courtney, McClellan, Kinmond, Bailey, Barrow, Brimage, Broadhead and Nerney and the Mrs. Smith, Winn, Bartlett, Hayward and Lucas coped cheerfully but efficiently with the slow but precise work involved in completing the OPSCAN forms, in particular the taxing work of assigning eight figure national grid references to at least two address items on each questionnaire and a maximum of four items in many cases.

Although the internal staff of a Project of this kind are very important, equally important are the companies who have consented to take part. In all, 43 organisations participated in the Follow-Up Survey and a further 35 organisations in the survey centred on five urban areas. Acceptance of our invitation to take part in the Project involved companies in giving both managerial time to a lengthy interview with myself or Mr. Duffett, as well as allowing every employee to receive our questionnaire and to take

time during their working day to complete it. At
no time did any of the organisations complain about
the amount of time which the exercise consumed, bearing
in mind that if each employee took ten minutes (probably
a minimum estimate) to complete our schedule then
in an office of 100 workers (assuming that all completed
the schedule) the equivalent of 17 man hours was taken
up by this task alone. In addition, the larger organisations devoted resources to organising the collection
and distribution of the questionnaires at different
departments or in different buildings (in one case).
This was always arranged efficiently and not without
additional cost to those companies which were anxious
to allow employees to retain their anonymity when
responding to the survey by returning their completed
questionnaires in envelopes provided by the company.
As a gesture of our appreciation of this considerable
investment of time and effort on the part of respondent
organisations a brief report on the results obtained
for each of them was made available.

Finally, the completion of this monograph would not have
been possible without the encouragement, understanding,
and patience of my wife and children, especially during
the last twelve months when the variety of tasks involved
in its preparation have become increasingly enmeshed
and have kept me at my desk in the Department well
after Paul and Charlotte would normally expect to
greet me home. I hope that I can now make up for
the time I owe them all.

Liverpool
October 1979   P.W.D.

1 Office location and the journey to work

INTRODUCTION

The relationship between homes and workplaces as expressed through the journey to work which links them has received a great deal of scrutiny.[1] There would be no useful purpose served by reviewing the standard references here; suffice to say that most of the studies undertaken have been confined to a single metropolitan area and/or have not focussed attention on the journey to work patterns generated by specific land uses.[2] The survey reported in this monograph therefore attempts a comparative study of travel to work in five urban areas with reference to one specific land use, namely office establishments. This is not the first time that office workers have been examined with reference to their journey to work; one of the most frequently cited major studies was undertaken in Chicago during the 1960s but it was largely confined to clerical workers who now comprise a diminishing proportion of all office workers.[3] The Location of Offices Bureau commissioned a comparative study of office worker journey to work travel in Liverpool, Central London and the Outer Metropolitan Area in 1966 but this was largely concerned with attitudes to work travel rather than objective differences between the study areas.[4] Wabe has also reported a study based on an office located in Epsom while a number of other studies of office workers have included some discussion of their journey to work.[5]

It is probably fair to say that rather more is known about aggregate patterns of movement generated by all land uses in cities than is known about their individual trip generation characteristics. The principal examples of an emphasis on aggregate analysis are the land use/transportation studies undertaken in large numbers during the 1960s and early 1970s.[6] These studies are an invaluable source of data on movement within individual towns and cities but it is usually difficult to compare the data collected because of the absence of any standardisation in both the range of information collected and the methods employed. There is still relatively limited information on traffic generation by the individual land uses which are represented in the zones usually employed as the framework for analysis in transportation studies. The study reported here is therefore an attempt to add to existing knowledge with respect to one land use which is providing accommodation for a growing proportion of all the

1

workers employed in urban areas.[7]   As a largely urban-
oriented activity, the volume of daily travel generated
by office buildings makes a critical contribution
to the overall volume of movement in towns and cities.
Detailed information about the effects of office employee
decisions on mode choice or participation in car sharing
for the journey to work is not simply valuable because
it supplements the aggregated data typical of transportation studies, it also assists an assessment of the
possible effects of alternative locations for office
space on the transport needs of existing and future
office development.[8]   While it has been shown that
the modal split and distances travelled vary in relation
to city size there are few studies which have examined
inter-urban variation in these characteristics for
the same land use.[9]

    It was this interest combined with the dominance
of office floorspace in central London which prompted
the Greater London Council (G.L.C.) to undertake a
study of the traffic generated by a sample of fifteen
office buildings which housed 91 firms in the City
of London, Camden, Westminster and Southwark. Detailed
surveys of all movements generated by the buildings
were undertaken on a normal weekday; visitor trips,
non-work trips during the lunch-hour, service vehicle
journeys and use of car parking spaces were all monitored
along with the journey to work trips in and out during
the day.[10]   A similar study was later undertaken in
suburban London using ten office buildings which provided
space for 48 firms in the London Boroughs of Croydon
Ealing and Enfield.[11]   There is one general conclusion
derived from both studies which is relevant to the
objectives of the present study. This relates to
the degree of variability in the trip generating characteristics of office buildings according to their location,
in particular the availability of car parking and
the level of service provided by public transport.
Both these factors were shown to influence the modal
split of work travel to the office buildings and to
indirectly affect the spatial and temporal attributes
of the work trips recorded in both surveys.

    In the central London study a distinct relationship
was also noted between place of work and place of
residence in a similar way to that observed in an
earlier study of office workers converging on the
Shell Building on the South Bank.[12]   Hence, City of
London office workers were found to travel predominantly
from east and south of central London while Camden
workers travelled mainly from the north and west sectors,
particularly from within the main built-up area of
Greater London.   It was also found that distances
and travel times for the journey to work varied according
to the mode of transport used and although rail commuters

travelled the furthest distances and took most time they
still had the most 'efficient' trips when the ratio
of median distance to median time is considered.[13]
Orrom and Wright have recently suggested that people's
choice of home in relation to their workplace is quite
efficient (in London) because it generates a volume
of travel which is close to the theoretical minimum
rather than to a volume generated by a random choice
of homes from the available stock.[14]

In both the G.L.C. studies it was also found that
public transport was extensively used over short distances
but the duration of travel was usually higher than
for journeys of equivalent distance by car. In the
suburban study it was also found that the distance
and duration of work trips was related to the scale
of employment concentration in the three suburbs with
Croydon, the largest centre for office employment,
having the highest average distances and journey times
and the lowest average speeds due to local congestion
and extensive local parking controls. The geographic
location of the office buildings in the suburban centres
also affected public transport modal split with bus
transport accommodating fewer journeys at buildings
with good rail/underground accessibility.

These and related findings are exclusively concerned
with the journey to work trips generated by office
buildings in a large metropolitan area but it remains
to be seen whether the relationship between the location
of office buildings and variations in trip generation
also apply to development in free-standing and much
smaller urban areas in other parts of Britain. The
range of alternative public transport modes in most
urban areas outside London is generally more limited
and largely confined to bus transport. By including
five urban areas at various distances from London
and at different positions in the urban hierarchy
this study provides an opportunity to see whether
these factors should be allowed for when attempting
to estimate the structure and characteristics of journey
to work travel generated by office buildings outside
London.

CONTEXT

The Office Decentralization Project was set up in
October 1975 to examine the travel to work and residential
location pattern of workers in offices which had decentralized from London between 1960 and 1969. As originally
conceived it was to be a follow-up survey of office
establishments used in a previous study by the author.[15]
It was not intended that it should include an examination
of the travel to work patterns of office workers in
groups of offices which had moved to a limited number

3

of contrasting urban areas.[16]   Soon after the project
commenced, however, it became clear that the results
of a survey based on individual decentralized offices
scattered at diverse locations throughout Britain
would make it difficult to assess the detailed impact
of several offices on travel to work patterns in reception
centres while also taking account of the differences
between urban areas in, for example, the density or
distribution of office development.   There are obvious
dangers attached to reaching conclusions about the
aggregate travel patterns of office staff in Glasgow
or Southampton on the basis of returns for only one
of several organisations which may have moved to these
centres.

In order to be rather more confident about measuring
the overall impact of relocated offices on travel
and housing demand in reception centres it therefore
seemed important to consider a few urban areas which
had received a substantial number of decentralized
offices and/or jobs since the initiatives introduced
during the early 1960s and to conduct a survey of
office establishments along lines similar to the Follow-
Up Survey.[17]   This part of the Project includes all
the offices which have moved to the selected urban
areas up to 1975.

The Project set out to examine three hypotheses.
These were specified as follows:

    I   Office workers employed in decentralized offices
        at the time of the 1969 survey have retained
        broadly similar journey to work and residential
        location patterns.

    II Replacement staff and new recruits in the 1969
        sample offices have not changed to any significant
        degree the journey to work and residential
        location patterns of decentralized office workers.

    III The detailed location characteristics of the
        1969 and 1976 sample offices, particularly
        with respect to accessibility by public transport,
        affects the balance between public and private
        transport trips for the present journey to
        work to decentralized offices.

There was also a fourth element in the brief which
was to look at the extent to which office decentralization
has added to pressure within the housing market of
the 'receiving' location.   In the event the Follow-
Up Survey proved most suitable for looking at Hypotheses
I and II.   This left the third hypothesis and the
question about housing demand only partially examined
in that survey, especially in the Part II report.

The four case study offices used in that report did not, however, provide a sufficiently wide range of transport conditions or locations to provide more conclusive evidence about the acceptability of hypothesis III. It was concluded that there does not appear to be a close relationship between the availability of transport sevices and the structure of journey to work travel to decentralized offices. It appears that other factors such as occupation structure or car ownership are more important influences on mode choice for the journey to work than the presence or absence of certain kinds of transport services.[18] The larger and more location-specific sample of office establishments used in the second part of the Project allows the validity of this result to be considered in more detail. A brief outline of the housing demand created by mobile office workers attached to decentralized offices was included in the Part II report. The brief analysis attempted there left a number of important questions unanswered and these included the temporal characteristics of the demand for housing accommodation in and around reception towns and the relationship between occupation status or previous workplace and spatial preferences for housing.

In addition to focussing on offices in a few urban areas, this part of the Project also has a different emphasis. In the Follow-Up Survey the principal question to be answered was whether the changes in journey to work behaviour which had been recorded in the earlier survey in 1969 continued to be evident some years later and, if not, in what direction were the more recent changes taking place. The theme of change in the journey to work is much less important in this comparative study of five urban areas and it will only be discussed in the context of travel mode choice and housing demand. The principal concern is to analyse the aggregate travel patterns of office workers in each of the study towns and to try to account for the differences between them by examining the location of the offices, the structure of the office labour force and the residential location choices made by office workers.

This is not to suggest that the results outlined should be viewed independently from the results of the Follow-Up Survey. The latter can usefully be used as a yardstick against which to compare the results from the survey towns and this is undertaken where it is believed that such comparisons may be useful. Most of the references will cite the 'Follow-Up Survey'.

The remainder of the monograph begins with a discussion of the characteristics of the survey towns and the offices which participated in the survey. This is followed in Chapter 3 by some comments on the recruitment of staff and the structure of the office labour force in the sample offices. There then follows a chapter which examines selected aspects of the demand for housing in and around each urban area, followed by chapters which deal, respectively, with the spatial and temporal attributes of the journey to work and with travel mode choice for the journey to work. This penultimate chapter also includes an attempt to account for the journey characteristics of office employees by reference to various socio-economic characteristics and the differences between the establishments included in the survey.

NOTES AND REFERENCES

(1) Some of the standard references include: J.D. Carroll, Jnr., 'The relation of homes to workplaces and the spatial pattern of cities', Social Forces, Vol. 30, 1952, pp. 271-82; H.S. Lapin, Structuring the Journey to Work, University of Pennsylvania Press, Philadelphia 1964; J.F. Kain, 'The journey to work as a determinant of residential location', Papers and Proceedings of the Regional Science Association, Vol. 9 1965; pp. 137-60; W.Y. Oi and P.W. Shuldiner, An Analysis of Urban Travel Demands, Northwestern University Press, Chicago 1962. For a more recent assessment see, for example, A.M. Guest and C. Cluett, 'Workplace and residential location: a push-pull model', Journal of Regional Science, Vol. 16, 1976, pp. 399-410. The relative importance of the journey to work in urban travel and its influence on urban form is illustrated in: M.F. Collins and T.M. Pharoah, Transport Organisation in a Great City: The Case of London, George Allen and Unwin, London 1974; M.J. Thomson, Great Cities and Their Traffic, Victor Gollanz, London 1977; K.H. Schaeffer and E. Sclar, Access for All: Transportation and Urban Growth, Penguin Books, Harmondsworth 1975; P.W. Daniels and A.M. Warnes, Movement in Cities: Perspectives on Urban Transport and Travel, Methuen, London 1980.

(2) A good example of an exception to this general rule is M.A. Taylor, Studies of Travel in Gloucester, Northampton and Reading, Report LR141, Road Research Laboratory, Crowthorne 1968.

(3) E.J. Taafe, B.J. Garner and M.H. Yeates, The Peripheral Journey to Work, Northwestern University Press, Evanston, 1963. The changing structure of the office labour force is shown in P.W. Daniels, Office Location: An Urban and Regional Study, Bell, London 1975.

(4) Location of Offices Bureau, White Collar Commuters: A Second Survey, Research Report No. 1, Location of Offices Bureau, London 1967.

(5) J.S. Wabe, 'Dispersal of employment and the journey to work', Journal of Transport Economics and Policy, Vol. 1, pp. 345-61. For a useful comparative study of the results of this and other studies of the journey to work by office workers see R.C. Harkness, 'Telecommunications Substitutes for Travel: A Preliminary Assessment of their Potential for Reducing Urban Transportation Costs by Altering Office Location Pattern', unpublished PhD. Thesis, University of Washington, Seattle, 1973, especially Ch. 4, pp. 149-337.

(6) The advantages and disadvantages of transportation studies are considered in D.N.M. Starkie, Transportation and Public Policy, Pergamon, Oxford 1973. See also W.Y. Oi and P.W. Shuldiner, op.cit.

(7) Details are given in R.B. Armstrong, The Office Industry, MIT Press, Boston 1972; P.W. Daniels (ed.), Spatial Patterns of Office Growth and Location, Wiley, London 1979.

(8) H.S. Lapin, op.cit., pp. 51-53.

(9) C.H. Townsley and J.L. Holloway, 'Surveys for office traffic generation studies', Department of Planning and Transportation Research Memorandum 385, Greater London Council, London 1973.

(10) J.L. Holloway, 'Traffic generation of central London offices', Department of Planning and Transportation Research Memorandum 399, Greater London Council, London 1974.

(11) C.H. Townsley, 'Traffic generation of suburban London offices', Department of Planning and Transportation Research Memorandum 398, Greater London Council, London 1973.

(12) Cited in J.T. Coppock, 'Dormitory settlements around London', in J.T. Coppock and H.C. Prince (eds.), Greater London, Faber, London 1964, p. 271. See also M.J.H. Mogridge, 'Some thoughts on the economics of intra-urban spatial location

of homes, worker residences and workplaces',
Proceedings of the Urban Economics Conference,
Centre for Environmental Studies, London 1973.

(13) J.L. Holloway, op.cit., p. 73.

(14) H.C. Orrom and C.C. Wright, 'The spatial distribution
of journey to work trips in Greater London',
Transportation, Vol. 5, 1976, pp. 192-222.

(15) P.W. Daniels, 'Office Decentralization from London:
The Journey to Work Consequences', unpublished
PhD. Thesis, University of London, 1972. See
also — , 'Transport changes generated by decentralized offices', *Regional Studies*, vol. 6, 1972,
pp. 273-89; — , 'Some changes in the journey
to work of decentralized office workers', *Town
Planning Review*, Vol. 44, 1973, pp. 167-88.

(16) The urban areas finally included are Watford,
Reading, Swindon, Southampton and Liverpool.
Further details are given in Chapter 2.

(17) The results of the Follow-Up Study are fully documen-
ted in P.W. Daniels, *A Follow-Up Study of the
Journey to Work to Decentralized Offices in
Britain: Final Report (Part I)* Departments
of Environment and Transport, London 1978; — ,
*Final Report (Part II) Case Studies at New Malden,
Southampton, Leicester and Durham*, Departments
of Environment and Transport, London 1978.

(18) The relationship between occupation status and
the journey to work is documented in: J.O. Wheeler,
'Occupational status and work trips: a minimum
distance approach', *Social Forces*, Vol. 45,
1967, pp. 508-15; — , 'Some affects of occupational
status on work trips', *Journal of Regional Science*,
Vol. 9, 1969, pp. 70-7; H.S. Lapin, op.cit.;
A. Hecht, 'The journey to work distance in relation
to the economic characteristics of workers',
Canadian Geographer, Vol. 18, 1974, pp. 367-
78; A.M. Guest, 'Occupation and the journey
to work', *Social Forces*, Vol. 55, 1976, pp.
166-81; L. Reeder, 'Social differentials in
mode of travel, time and cost in the journey
to work', *American Sociological Review*, Vol.
21, 1956, pp. 56-63; C.A. Murawski and D.E.
Boyce, 'Variation in urban work trip length
by mode, location and worker characteristics',
Transportation Research, Vol. 12, 1978, pp.
97-110.

2 The survey towns and participant office establishments

SELECTION OF SURVEY TOWNS

The five towns included in this study were selected
from a short list of eight centres which, according
to Location of Offices Bureau and other records, had
received several decentralized offices during the period
since 1960. An additional criterion was that any centre
included in the short list should have a reasonable
balance between pre- and post- 1969 migrant offices of
both large and small firms (less than fifty employees).
There should also be some locational contrasts in the
list because it had been observed in earlier research
that there appeared to be some variation in the journey
to work behaviour of office workers in different parts
of the country.[1] After discussing the preliminary list
with the Department of the Environment it was agreed
that the five centres for which details are given in
Table 2.1 would be used for the study.

Some 10,500 jobs had been moved to, or had been created
in, the five centres by 87 decentralized offices during
the period up to the end of 1975 (Table 2.1). Most
of the offices are in the private sector with civil
service departments accounting for less than 10 percent
of the total jobs. Only Southampton and Liverpool have
a significant proportion of the latter and there are
no offices in this category in Watford and Swindon while
they comprise only a very minor share (one office and
18 jobs) in Reading. The balance between pre- and post-
1969 decentralized offices in the private sector is
very even but in terms of jobs the post-1969 movers
have introduced almost twice as many jobs as the pre-
1969 movers. There is some evidence, therefore, that
larger offices have been choosing to move into these
urban areas as office decentralization activity reached
its peak during the early 1970s.[2] The local transport
effects of more recent office relocation to the study
towns can therefore be expected to be more wide ranging
than they were in the late 1960's when relatively few
offices had moved. This is particularly important for
Reading where only 263 jobs had been added to the local
economy by decentralized offices in the years prior
to 1969 compared with 2,460 during the period after
1969. This dichotomy is also apparent to some degree
in Swindon but in Watford the situation is reversed
and there has been a declining rate of job growth attributable to decentralizing firms since 1969. In Southampton the contribution of firms to office employment

9

Table 2.1

Summary data for the survey towns

		Watford	Reading	Swindon	Southampton	Liverpool	Total
(I) COMMERCIAL OFFICES							
Moved Pre-1969	A	10	11	4	8	5	38
	B	6	10	0	6	4	26
	C	4	1	4	2	1	12
	D	1034	263	1147	534	223	3201
Moved Post-1969	A	11	14	6	8	3	42
	B	9	9	1	5	1	25
	C	2	5	5	3	2	17
	D	426	2460	1559	598	937	5980
(II) CIVIL SERVICE OFFICES							
Moved 1963–72	A	–	1	–	3	3	7
	B	–	1	–	–	–	1
	C	–	–	–	3	3	6
	D	–	18	–	947	403	1368
TOTALS (I + II)	A	21	26	10	16	11	87
	B	15	19	1	11	5	52
	C	6	7	9	5	6	35
	D	1460	2741	2706	2079	1563	10549

Continued .....

Table 2.1 (continued)

	Watford	Reading	Swindon	Southampton	Liverpool	Total
OTHER CHARACTERISTICS						
1	0.4	9.4	1.4	1.1	4.2	1.9
2	Yes	Yes	Yes	Yes	Yes	
3	No	No	No	No	No	
4	30.0	30.5	23.9*	29.4*	28.7*	28.5
5	M	M	OSE	OSE	P	
6	78,465	132,939	91,033	209,580	610,113	
7	47,280	73,250	46,810	111,570	324,840	
8	588.6	1,369.9	359.9	1,690.2	8,662.8	

Notes:

A – No. of firms

B – No. employing less than 50 staff

C – No. employing more than 50 staff

D – Total jobs

1. Ratio of post-to pre-1969 commercial sector offices

2. Co-operative local government offices

3. Department of Employment Survey

4. % office occupation by workplace (1966). * 1971 Census

5. Location:

   M – Metropolitan Region
   OSE – Outer South East
   P – Provincial

6. Total resident population, 1971

7. Total persons with workplaces in each centre, 1971

8. Commercial office floorspace (thousand sq. ft.), 1967

growth in both periods is more or less identical (see Table 2.1).

OFFICE DEVELOPMENT IN THE SURVEY TOWNS

Watford has benefited greatly from the rapid expansion of office and service employment in the South Hertford-shire area as a whole which is very accessible to London and has an expanding and relatively affluent population.[3] Hertfordshire has experienced growth of office employment (particularly in free standing office buildings) at a rate considerably above the national average. This is exemplified by insurance, banking and finance which between 1959 and 1969 increased its employment by 8.4 percent in Hertfordshire compared with 3.1 percent nation-ally, or public administration, 3.4 percent in Hertford-shire and 1.2 percent in Great Britain. During the 1960's the county council's policies towards primary office development had been permissive and decentral-ization of offices was allowed to centres such as Welwyn Garden City, Stevenage or Royston but Watford was not included; a subsidiary part of policy was concerned to limit the growth of office space in Watford. This arose from the pressure of demand for office space which was largely concentrated on centres in the southern half of the county. More restrictive policies were subsequently introduced with a view to limiting the growth of offices to a level that seemed acceptable in relation to the anticipated growth of office worker labour supply and from the population growth envisaged under the policies. Office permissions in Watford were restricted to offices serving local markets such as estate agents, accountants or locally oriented offices of central government departments.

Despite this early policy of containment, Watford has consistently experienced considerable pressure for new office development and 1 mill. sq. ft. were granted permission (mainly in large developments) between March 1972 and March 1974 alone. Most of the refusals, amounting to 850,000 sq. ft. during the same period, involved large scale office buildings. This continuing high level of provision in Watford, in spite of the restrictive policies, is a by-product of earlier large scale permissions which in 1975 were still being implemented. The employment growth connected with this development has occurred principally in the financial services sector as well as in ancillary offices attached to manufacturing plants throughout the Watford area. Although it is the smallest centre (in terms of population) included in this study, Watford is not a free-standing town; it is only 18 miles north west of central London with which it has good British Rail as well as London Transport underground connections. Its potential labour catchment area therefore extends well into the contiguous areas of north west London

12

and is much larger than the adminstratively based population statistic indicates.

Only 22 minutes from Paddington by British Rail's high speed train, Reading does not seem seriously disadvantaged by being 39 miles from central London and it is now part of one of the most rapidly growing areas in the South East. During the decade prior to the survey undertaken in 1976, Reading had developed into one of the principal free-standing centres in the Outer Metropolitan Area (OMA). Apart from its accessibility to London by rail, London (Heathrow) Airport is conveniently accessible via the M4 motorway so that Reading is also an important interchange point. It comprises part of the area designated in the Strategic Plan for the South East as suitable for major long term growth (Reading - Wokingham - Aldershot - Basingstoke).[4] The structure plan for central Berkshire had not been completed by 1976 and it was therefore necessary for the County to review office policy for Reading and to set down criteria to be used in assessing applications for office development prior to the completion of the Central Berkshire Structure Plan.[5] The pre-reorganisation Reading Borough Council placed a limit on permitted office floorspace (1971-81) of 1.5 mill. sq. ft. because it anticipated high levels of demand following possible relaxation of office development permit (ODP) controls which were due to expire in 1972. A preferred zone for office development in the city centre extending west from the railway station along King's Road was also specified (the area in which the majority of the offices in the 1976 survey are located). Application of the floorspace ceiling and the preferred zone strategy did not prove very successful and a further review of office policy was undertaken in 1973 which resulted in a very restrictive policy (adopted in March 1974) for the central area (as well as the remainder of the Borough). In essence, this was designed to ensure that outstanding planning permissions were used, that the growth of local firms would not be jeopardised, and that major developments both outside and inside the preferred zone would be reviewed.

In common with the effects of ODP policy on the central London office market, a virtually complete embargo on office development in Reading during 1974/75 hit particularly hard at small local office employers wanting to locate or to expand in the town. It also created a shortage of good office floorspace so that rents were pushed upwards and sites already cleared in anticipation of office development were left as open and unsightly gaps in the built fabric of the central area. Thus the policy was again examined

in 1975 and a rather more flexible approach was substituted with a view to minimising the negative consequences of the previous policy and to achieving
some planning gains from the office development which
was approved. The need to apply this policy carefully
in the light of a shortage of office labour in central
Berkshire was also noted.

Swindon is one of the best examples of successful
participation in the town expansion programme under
the auspices of the Town Development Act 1952.[6] The
policy of the Borough of Thamesdown (of which Swindon
is now a part) is therefore concerned primarily with
attracting sufficient investment and diversity of
employment to match the growth of population connected
with the expansion programme.[7] In contrast to Reading,
Swindon has always remained outside the control area
for ODPs (some 79 miles from central London) and this,
combined with the availability of housing, has attracted
some major office employers. Swindon also has good
communications by road (M4) and rail (HST) with London
and its central position in southern England makes
it a convenient place for distribution or for controlling
offices and plants located elsewhere in the country.
Much of the new office development has been located
outside the central area and has created a distribution
of office development which is rather different to
the other study towns and which may well be reflected
in the journey to work patterns discussed later.
In 1975 further growth of office employment was expected
to account for 25 percent of the net increase in jobs
in Swindon and most of it will be accommodated in
buildings outside the town centre.

OTHER STUDIES

There have been very few other studies which can be
used as a basis for comparison with the results of
this survey. As far as the author is aware the only
study which is directly relevant is work undertaken
by Economic Consultants for the Location of Offices
Bureau in 1971.[8] Watford was one of the centres included
in a study of the demand and supply for office workers
and the local impact of office development using survey
and Census material. The field survey in Watford
involved contact with eight individual offices all
of which were in-migrants to the major office developments
completed in Watford up to 1971. Most of the firms
had moved there between 1966 and 1970 although one
had moved as far back as 1955. Information about
employee recruitment and the journey to work was sought
from staff in the offices participating in the survey
and will be cited for comparative purposes where appropriate.

THE PARTICIPANT OFFICES AND THEIR LOCATION

A total of 74 organisations were approached to participate in the survey and 38 finally agreed to provide assistance (Table 2.2). A large number of companies included in our primary listings had in fact moved away or had ceased to trade and the proportion of straight refusals was approximately 25 percent. The best overall response from the organisations approached was obtained in Swindon where five out of eight possibilities agreed to assist; the least satisfactory response was achieved in Watford where only eight out of nineteen eligible organisations eventually agreed to take part in the study.

The offices taking part in the survey are mainly from the service sector (Fig. 2.1) and this was also the case in the parallel follow-up survey.[9] The distributive trades are well represented in the sample as a whole along with professional and scientific services which together account for 37 percent of the offices in the survey. Insurance, banking and finance offices are less well represented than would be expected on the basis of their important contribution to decentralization while public administration and defence are also under represented compared with the follow-up survey where they accounted for over 23 percent of the 42 offices included. The industrial classification of the respondent offices in each individual town coincides quite well with the overall distribution with the exception of Swindon where manufacturing sector offices are not represented. The Swindon respondents are dominated by the distributive trades with over half of the organisations in this category in the sample as a whole located there. Reading has the most diverse range of decentralized offices; only public utilities, distributive trades and public administration are under-represented.

Almost half of the establishments in the survey are headquarters offices with regional offices forming the second most important group (Fig. 2.2). Swindon is again distinctive in that it has the most polarised distribution with three head offices and two 'sectons' of head offices out of the six decentralized offices sampled. In Watford, on the other hand, all the categories listed in Fig. 2.2 occur, except sole offices. In all the other towns head offices account for between 40 and 50 percent of the sample.

Detailed statistics for the number of employees and their response rates in the decentralized offices in each town are given in Table 2.2. The procedures used to gather journey to work information for individual office workers were identical to those utilized in

Table 2.2
Office response rates in the survey towns

Town	Office no.	Total employees	Total respondents	% Response
WATFORD	(91)	16	11	68.8
	(22)F[1]	29	18	62.1
	(96)	369	216	58.5
	(80)	288	157	54.5
	(82)	37	18	48.7
	(88)	23	11	47.8
	(95)	55	11	20.0
Sub-total	7	819	442	54.1
READING	(86)	9	9	100.0
	(76)	38	32	84.2
	(78)	9	7	78.8
	(87)	39	27	69.2
	(77)	32	22	68.8
	(64)	77	48	62.3
	(75)	36	21	58.3
	(90)	1,179	562	47.7
	(84)	1,095	409	37.4
	(93)	594	213	35.9
	(68)	48	16	33.3
Sub-total	11	3,156	1,366	43.3
SWINDON	(92)	83	67	76.1
	(38)F	64	37	57.8
	(79)	200	83	41.5
	(74)	1,359	544	40.3
	(89)**[2]	332	118	35.5
	(85)	919	234	25.5
Sub-total	6	2,957	1,083	36.6
SOUTHAMPTON	(73)	27	27	100.0
	(97)	17	13	76.5
	(69)	27	20	74.1
	(67)**	72	53	73.6
	(47)F**	260	174	66.9
	(98)**	107	67	62.6
	(65)	250	113	45.2
	(66)	100	39	39.0
	(72)	325	117	36.0
Sub-total	9	1,185	623	52.6
LIVERPOOL	(70)	22	13	59.1
	(71)	125	59	47.2
	(83)	732	206	28.1
	(19)**	103	21	20.4

Continued ......

Table 2.2 (continued)

Town	Office no.	Total employees	Total respondents	% Response
Sub-total	4	982	·299	30.4
Grand total	37	9,097	3,813	41.9

Notes: 1.   Offices included in Follow-Up Survey 1976

2.   Offices of central government or nationalised industries

Source: Office Survey, 1976.

17

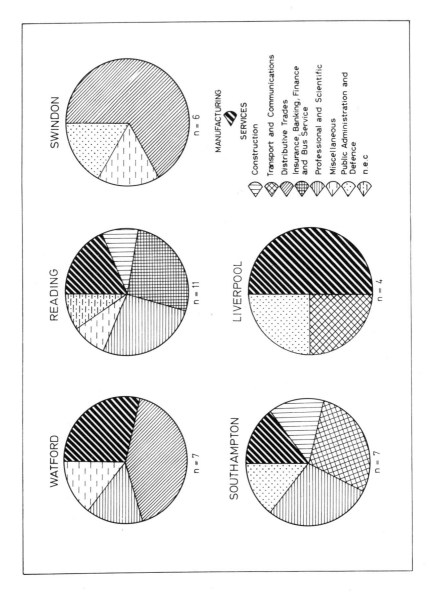

SWINDON n = 6

READING n = 11

WATFORD n = 7

LIVERPOOL n = 4

SOUTHAMPTON n = 7

MANUFACTURING

SERVICES

Construction
Transport and Communications
Distributive Trades
Insurance Banking, Finance and Bus Service
Professional and Scientific
Miscellaneous
Public Administration and Defence
n.e.c

Figure 2.1   Respondent offices in each centre by standard industrial classification.

18

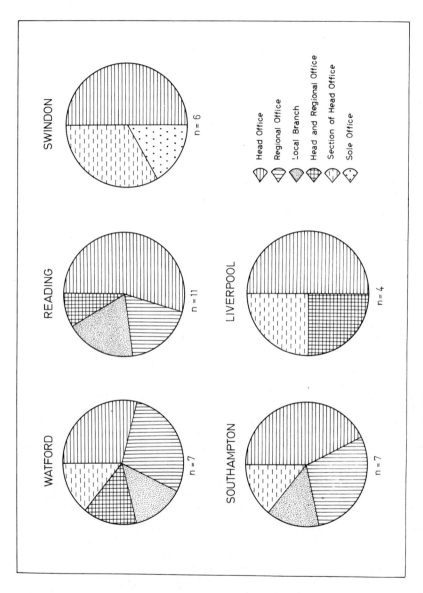

SWINDON n = 6

READING n = 11

WATFORD n = 7

LIVERPOOL n = 4

SOUTHAMPTON n = 7

Head Office
Regional Office
Local Branch
Head and Regional Office
Section of Head Office
Sole Office

Figure 2.2 Organisational status of respondent offices in each centre.

the Follow-Up Study and involved each office distributing a questionnaire (identical to that used in the other survey, see Appendix) to each of their employees. An important reason for retaining this procedure was cost even though it was recognised that the exercise would generate data referring to previous travel behaviour which was not required for this particular part of the research programme. It was not considered feasible to institute follow-up procedures for non-respondents because of the problems of identifying such individuals and the prospect of further impositions on organisational time and goodwill. The response rates given in Table 2.2 are therefore the product of the one-off attempt to obtain journey to work information.

Small employers with less than 50 staff account for almost 43 percent of the respondents in the cluster towns but at the same time very large employers with more than 800 office staff are also well represented. Intermediate categories are more unevenly distributed with offices employing 101-200 and 401-800 staff under-represented. The size distribution of offices in each study town therefore clearly affects the total number of employees comprising the sample population so that although Watford has one more office than Swindon this amounts to just 819 staff compared with 2,957 in Swindon _where there are two companies employing more than 800 office staff. A similar situation exists at Reading where 75 percent of tne employers have less than 50 office staff but three have more than 400. The most even distribution of office sizes (by employment) occurs in Southampton, although very large employers are under-represented.

The office with the median response rate of 57.8 percent is located in Swindon (office 38) and if the list for those establishments which achieved a better return rate is examined only three offices (47, 98, 96) had more than one hundred employees. Yet fourteen of the nineteen firms below the median office had more than one hundred employees in 1976. Three of these were substantial employers with well over 1,000 employees, but they only generated response rates of 47.7 percent, 40.3 percent, and 37.4 percent respect- ively. The relatively poor returns from these three establishments obviously has a marked influence on the overall response rates from the survey towns. Though it should be noted in this instance that, unlike the Follow-Up Survey, none of the really large establishments are in the central government sector. Indeed the latter group of offices are relatively unimportant in the sample and only represent thirteen percent of the offices and nine percent of the employees. When one compares response rates for each centre both Southampton (52.6 percent) and Watford (54.1 percent) achieved a reasonable quota of returned schedules, with Reading (43.3 percent) falling a little behind the Follow-Up Survey's 47 percent whilst Swindon (36.6 percent) and Liverpool (30.4 percent) produced much poorer figures. In many ways the results obtained from Southampton, Watford and Reading parallel closely those produced at the same time by the offices in the Follow-Up Survey. The response rates in many Reading offices are better than the impression given by the overall percentage; Southampton with the highest figure has two-thirds of its response rates above the median office, Reading has exactly the same proportion of offices above this divide. However, with the exception of one of these establishments, all the offices concerned employ less than forty staff. Three of the four firms in Reading below the median are all very large employers. The latter has undoubtedly weighted the Reading response towards the unfavourable range since it might otherwise have achieved a rate equal to or better than the Follow-Up Survey. The fairly poor response for Swindon is given added emphasis when it is observed that only one of the six offices comes above the median.

These results illustrate the importance of office size as a diagnostic indicator of response rates, since the two smallest Swindon offices had the best return rates. Nevertheless, the internal organisation of an office and the motivation of the staff distributing the schedules may also have a significant influence on employees' willingness to return completed question-naires. For example, at one large office in Swindon the management explained the purpose of the survey to their employees as well as hand-stamping every question-naire with a label indicating at which of the two sites they occupied the schedules were distributed. This care and attention is possibly reflected in the reponse rate of forty percent from 1359 employees which is one of the better results from large private sector establishments. The structure of employment in an office may also affect the response rate; some 64 percent of the employees at office 90 in Reading are in managerial or professional grades and these are more likely to complete schedules than clerical workers. Hence it has a high response rate when compared with other firms of an equivalent size. The occupational balance of employees can be important in another way: it was noted in the 1969 survey that clerical workers were more prone to refuse en masse to complete question-naires, if for example, one particularly strong-willed and personable individual in a typing pool objected to the contents of the questionnaire schedules. The distribution of response from the Watford office is somewhat eccentric, with two offices, including the fairly large office 96 being above the median position and three firms of varying size lying in a group immediately below the median office. The other two Watford offices are left trailing at the end of the frequency distribution with response rates of only twenty-two and twenty percent. Part of the explanation for the poor response from one of these offices may be due to the contact mode used. Office 81 is a subtenant of office 80 and the latter offered to organise the survey and explain its purpose to its tenant. Perhaps because the management of this company were never personally approached and interviewed by Project staff, they were not prepared to motivate their employees to complete their schedules.

Reference must also be made to the very poor results achieved in Liverpool (30.4 percent), a surprisingly low figure when it is considered that the survey was organised from a local education institution. Only one of the four offices which constituted this group, the smallest, produced a response rate above the median level. Although the shipping company (office 71) has a reasonable quota of returned schedules (42.2 percent), the response from the much larger office 83 is extremely disappointing (28.1 percent). The reasons for the poor results in Liverpool are not known but it does make it more difficult to compare with any confidence the data obtained in this centre with those produced by the three leading towns in terms of response rates, Southampton, Watford and Reading.

Office floorspace occupied is largely a direct reflection of employment levels so that 37 percent of the respondents occupy less than 10,000 sq. ft. (gross) and 26 percent occupy more than 70,000 sq. ft. (Fig. 2.3). There again appears to be stronger polarisation in the sample than is the case in the Follow-Up Study in which intermediate floorspace groups are better represented. Swindon again emerges as a distinctive centre with four large office premises exceeding 45,000 sq. ft.

LOCATION OF OFFICES IN SURVEY TOWNS

Maps have been prepared to show the location of the respondent offices in relation to the principal road network and transport services of each centre (Fig. 2.4 - 2.8). This information will be used later in the context of the travel to work attributes of office workers and to establish whether presence/absence of public transport services, in particular, is at least a contributory factor to the modal structure of work trips. It was not possible to ensure contrasting intra-urban office location patterns from the outset

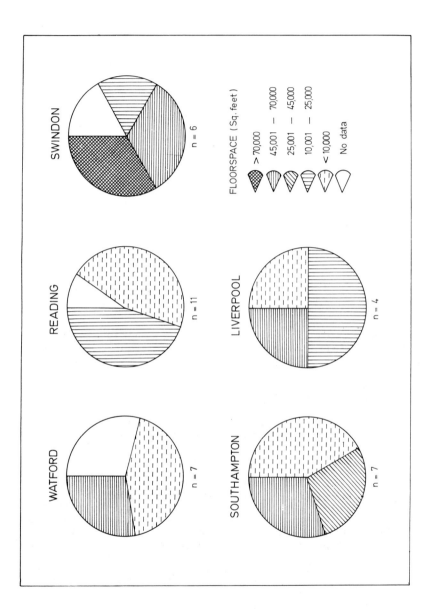

Figure 2.3 Floorspace size of survey offices.

because of the uncertainty about response but the final distribution of participant offices reveals highly contrasting spatial patterns which range from a nucleated (or centralized) distribution in Watford (Fig. 2.4) to a very dispersed (or decentralized) location pattern for the offices which have located in Swindon (Fig. 2.6). In the three other centres the location patterns of the respondent offices are more conveniently classified as intermediate and are typified by a combination of highly centralized and partially decentralized locations. In the case of Liverpool (Fig. 2.8) the size of the sample makes it difficult to describe the location pattern in these general terms since two of the offices are in the city centre, one is located in a competing suburban centre (Bootle) and the other is attached to a manufacturing plant in the inner city but some distance from the central area (Old Swan).

All but one of the offices in Watford (Fig. 2.4) are located in or near to the Clarendon Road area which extends due south from the railway station which is served by British Rail mainline services from Bletchley to Euston and suburban services from Watford to Euston and t he London Transport underground (Bakerloo line) to central London. This means that all the offices are located within half a mile of rail services.. The exception is office 95 which is on a trading estate outside the centre of Watford and is not easily accessible except by a limited bus service and by private transport. Because of the highly centralized distribution bus services from a wide range of areas inside and outside Watford are also within easy walking distance of most of the offices.

This is not the situation in Reading (Fig. 2.5) where, apart from the six establishments located in the town centre, the offices are more widely dispersed on or near routes which are served by one or only a limited number of bus services from particular areas inside or outside the town. There is the additional problem in Reading of cross-movement from north or south of the River Thames which is only facilitated by two road bridges which become highly congested during peak periods and probably reduce the attractiveness of public transport for work trips. Two of the offices in the sample (68 and 78) are on the north side of the river, somewhat isolated from the transport connections which focus on the central area on the southern side of the river. Particularly advantageous for some of the offices in this sample will be access to Reading British Rail station which, in two cases, is within 50 yards of the premises (64 and 90), and is within easy walking distance (¼ mile) for three others (75, 87, and 84). Office 93 is less accessible

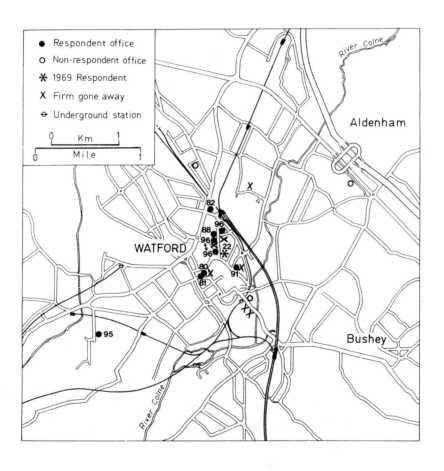

Figure 2.4   Location of respondent and non-respondent
             offices in Watford.

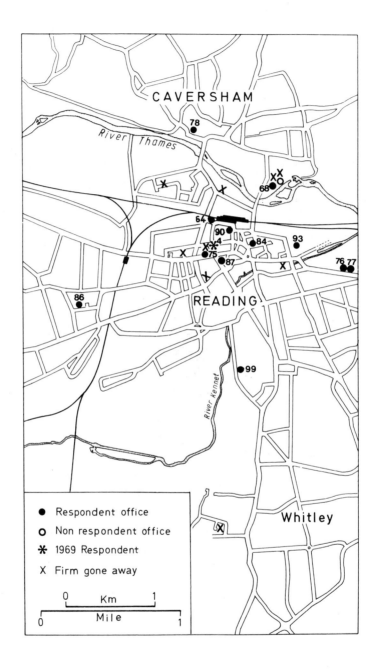

Figure 2.5 Location of respondent and non-respondent
offices in Reading.

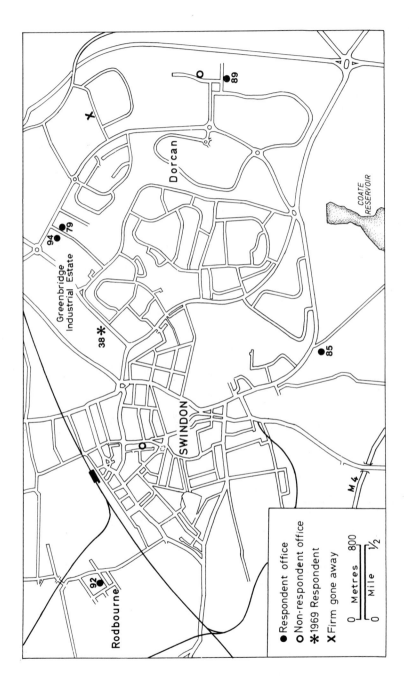

Figure 2.6 Location of respondent and non-respondent offices in Swindon.

27

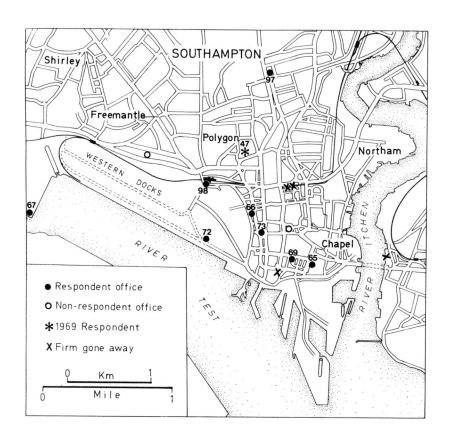

Figure 2.7   Location of respondent and non-respondent
offices in Southampton.

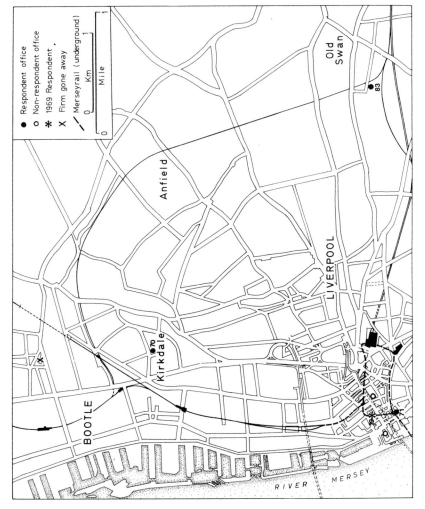

Legend:
- ● Respondent office
- ○ Non-respondent office
- ＊ 1969 Respondent .
- ✗ Firm gone away
- ╱ Merseyrail (underground)

0 — Km — 1
0 — Mile — 1

Old Swan

83

Anfield

LIVERPOOL

Kirkdale

70

BOOTLE

RIVER MERSEY

Figure 2.8 Location of respondent and non-respondent offices in Liverpool.

29

than its location adjacent to the main line suggests and it will be interesting to see whether this is reflected in the journey to work. For the remaining offices the station is at least one mile distant and users would probably need to use an intermediate mode (apart from walking) to get to and from their places of work.

The most decentralized location pattern occurs in Swindon (Fig. 2.6) where all the offices are positioned well towards the outer limits of the built-up area and are mostly some distance from each other. The assessment of travel to work behaviour in Swindon will therefore be concerned rather less with the availability of rail and bus services and more with whether the relatively independent locations (apart from offices 74 and 79) of the sample establishments generate journey to work advantages such as more restricted trip time distributions, more compact labour catchment areas, and higher than average frequencies of journeys to work on foot. It would also seem likely that the congestion caused by agglomeration of office establishments is not an important consideration in Swindon although local congestion caused by inadequate capacity of access roads to individual offices does apparently occur (e.g. office 85).

The distribution of respondent offices in Southampton (Fig. 2.7) is perhaps the most diverse for the five centres used in this survey. There are offices located in the heart of the central area (73 and 69); an office located immediately above the main line British Rail station (98), two offices (72 and 67) which are located on the waterfront in the Western Docks area; and an office (97) which is isolated from the central area and city-serving public transport services. Offices 67, 72 and 97 are, however, free of the traffic congestion and parking difficulties complained of by office 47. All the offices, except one, are located beyond easy walking distance (½ mile) of the main line station but are, with the notable exception of offices 72 and 67, accessible to a variety of bus services serving the central area.

Some comment has already been made about the location of the Liverpool offices (Fig. 2.8). It should also be noted that the Loop and Link underground line which provides improved interchange facilities was not operational between suburban and main line services into the central area in the summer of 1976 when the data was collected. Both the Kirkdale (7) and Old Swan (83) offices are served primarily by radial bus routes and rail services do not offer a viable alternative for the journey to work in either case.

ACCESS TO OFFICES BY PUBLIC AND PRIVATE TRANSPORT

Some of the features outlined for each centre are summarised in Table 2.3 which collates the responses to a number of questions presented to office managements about travel facilities to their establishments. Although Swindon has a highly decentralized pattern of office development this has not been at the expense of the availability of accessible bus services but at Southampton, where the pattern is certainly more centralized, almost half of the managers interviewed claimed that their premises were not easily accessible to local bus services. A by-product of the location pattern in Swindon, however, is that half the offices participate in some kind of special arrangement with local bus operators in order to cope with the problems of assembling large numbers of staff from diverse locations. Clearly bus stops within easy walking distance do not convey an indication of the range and quality of the service provided and it is inevitable that, in Swindon's case, it is likely to be restricted. Arrangements with local bus operators are less frequent in three of the other centres and the one example in Watford involves an office (95) which is clearly isolated from the central area and the principal bus routes. Such arrangements appear to be the exception rather than the rule. Only two offices operate their own minibus services, both in Southampton, and these have been introduced because of the total absence of public transport services (offices 67 and 72). There are some licencing difficulties with these arrangements, however, and in one case office staff apparently prefer to use their own transport wherever possible (office 67).

Respondents to the management questionnaire were also invited to comment on public transport services to and from their offices and most of them emphasised the negative aspects. The effects of congestion on the quality of bus services was often mentioned by the offices in Reading along with the poor services from outside the main built-up area and the high costs of using them. On the other hand one office (90), which is well positioned for bus and rail services described trains and local bus services as reasonable. In view of the location pattern, it is not perhaps surprising that congestion was not remarked upon by respondents in Swindon; of rather more concern was the limiting coverage and structure of bus services and the costs and limitations which these impose on residential location choice, especially for office staff from households which only have one car. Journeys from villages and towns outside the main built-up area of Swindon are particularly difficult but the services also restrict the possibilities of attracting

31

Table 2.3

Summary of transport services to/from survey offices

Public transport services	Watford Yes	No	NI[1]	Reading Yes	No	NI	Survey Town Swindon Yes	No	NI	Southampton Yes	No	NI	Liverpool Yes	No	NI	Total Yes	No	NI
Parking space for visitors	6	1	-	5	4	2	4	1	1	3	4	-	1	2	1	19	12	4
Car sharing encouraged	-	2	(5)[2]	-	8	(3)	3	1	(2)	1	2	(4)	-	2	(2)	4	15	(16)
Bus stops within easy walking distance	3	1	3	11	-	-	5	-	1	4	3	-	4	-	-	27	4	4
Access to tube and/or BR	3	1	3	6	4	1	3	1	2	4	3	-	2	2	-	18	11	6
Arrangement with local bus company	1	6	-	-	11	-	3	2	1	1	6	-	1	3	-	6	28	1
Company minibus service	-	7	-	-	11	-	-	5	1	2	5	-	-	4	-	2	32	1

Notes: 1. No information provided

2. Organisations did not have a policy for encouraging car-sharing or had not considered the matter before it was mentioned to them at the interview.

Source: Management Questionnaire, 1976.

staff from households which do not have any private transport available.

The most recurrent comment about public transport in Watford is its unreliability and the way in which buses are taken off routes without any prior warning, thus imposing delays on the journey to work of office staff. The cost of the public transport was also considered too high. The comments of the Southampton respondents are not clearly focused on particular problems common to all the respondent offices. Difficulties encounted by particular offices seem to arise mainly from their particular location circumstances and perhaps would not occur if they occupied similar premises elsewhere. Congestion in the central area is probably the principal concern of offices in and around that area, especially its effect on the operation of the bus lanes. At office 90 employees get the first eight miles of rail travel free and then pay for journeys beyond this distance so that there is more incentive to avoid peak hour travel problems on the roads altogether. The managers of the offices in Liverpool did not have any comments to make on local public transport services.

Two other factors which are likely to affect the overall number and structure of the journey to work trips generated by the offices in the survey towns are also included in Table 2.3. One-third of the offices able to provide information on availability of parking space for visitors do not have these facilities, particularly in Southampton and Reading. Despite their highly centralized location pattern all but one of the Watford offices are able to provide parking space for visitors. Of more direct relevance to the journey to work, however, is the attitude of office organisations towards car sharing which has gained increasing prominence since the energy crisis of 1973.[10] Only four of the 19 offices with a positive view actually encouraged it and almost half of the organisations had not thought about it prior to the interview even though the earlier fuel crisis had generated publicity for schemes which encouraged employees and their organisations to reduce energy costs by pooling trips by private transport as far as practicable. This result is interesting since one in three of the offices in the Follow-Up Survey which had a definte policy encouraged car sharing but only one in four of the offices in the five study towns. Not one of the offices in Liverpool, Watford and Reading encouraged car sharing but three of four offices in Swindon did so. It is possible. that this is a by-product of the location pattern of office premises in the latter; elsewhere the level of centraility had made the case for car sharing less obvious.

Table 2.4

Number of parking spaces at survey offices

No. of spaces	Survey towns					Total		Follow-Up Survey	
	Watford	Reading	Swindon	Southampton	Liverpool	No.	%	No.	%
< 25	5	6	–	5	1	17	48.6	9	20.9
26 – 50	–	–	1	1	–	2	5.7	11	25.6
51 – 100	1	1	1	–	–	3	8.6	4	9.3
101 – 200	–	2	1	1	1	5	14.3	5	11.6
> 200	1	1	2	–	1	5	14.3	6	14.0
Non-response	–	–	1	–	–	1	2.9	5	11.6
Not applicable	–	1	–	–	1	2	5.7	3	7.0
Total	7	11	6	7	4	35	100	43	100
Total spaces	259	1231	1514	274	862	4140	–	–	–
No. employees per space	3.0	2.7	3.1	3.3	1.1	2.5	–	–	–

Source: Management Questionnaire, 1976

The managers also provided information on the number of parking spaces (Table 2.4) and, apart from Liverpool, the ratio of employees to parking spaces available within the office curtilage is very uniform and ranges between 2.7 and 3.3 employees per space. In general there is a direct relationship between number of employees and parking space and the distribution shown in Table 2.4 conforms quite closely with the distribution of offices by number of employees (Table 2.2). The office car park is the first choice of the staff of at least 80 percent of the offices but in some cases it is not possible to satisfy the demand for parking space by only using the facilities within office curtilages. The principal alternative, in common with the Follow-Up survey, is a ground level car park within walking distance. Free on-street parking is also used in Reading and Southampton but was only mentioned by one office in Swindon where office parking shortages might have been expected to encourage the overflow of demand into adjacent residential streets.

A large number of respondents commented on the in-adequacy of parking provision and most are concerned about the relationship between supply and demand. Excess demand for existing spaces is principally a difficulty in Reading and Southampton with only one office in Swindon mentioning the inadequancy of parking facilities. A number of firms are anxious to increase the number of spaces available but they are not very optimistic about local authority attitudes or the willingness of their landlords to provide additional space. More general problems connected with access to office premises by private transport were much fewer than those for public transport and local traffic congestion affecting traffic flows into and out of premises seems to be the only problem (cf. Swindon, office 79).

NOTES AND REFERENCES

(1)   P.W. Daniels, 'Office Decentralization from London: The Journey to Work Consequences', unpublished Ph.D. Thesis, University of London 1972.

(2)   Location of Offices Bureau, Office Relocation : Facts and Figures, Location of Offices Bureau, London 1975, pp. 6-7.

(3)   Hertfordshire County Council, Offices: A Comparison of Trends and Policy, 1971-74, County Planning Department, Hertford 1975.

(4)   South East Economic Planning Council, Strategic Plan for South East, Her Majesty's Stationery Office, London 1967.

(5)   Royal County of Berkshire and Reading Borough
      Council, Offices in the Area of Reading Borough
      Council: An Interim Strategic Policy Statement,
      County and District Planning Departments, Newbury,
      and Reading 1979.

(6)   M. Harloe, Swindon: A Town in Transition, Heinemann,
      London 1975.   See also, I.H. Seeley, Planned
      Expansion of Country Towns, George Godwin,
      London 1968.

(7)   Borough of Thamesdown, 'Employment', Corporation
      Planning Information Report OP3, Swindon 1975.

(8)   See Location of Offices Bureau, Demand and Supply
      for Office Workers and the Local Impact of
      Office Development.   A report prepared for
      the Bureau by Economic Consultants Ltd., Location
      of Offices Bureau, London 1971.

(9)   More details are given in A.W. Duffett and P.W.
      Daniels, The Journey to Work at Decentralized
      Offices in Britain - (1) A Follow-Up Study
      (2) at Groups of Offices in Watford, Reading,
      Swindon, Southampton and Liverpool: Final Report
      Part IV - Survey Design, Data Processing and
      Analysis, Departments of Environment and Transport,
      London 1979.

(10) P.W. Daniels, 'Vehicle sharing for the journey
      to work by office workers', forthcoming paper
      recently submitted to Traffic Engineering and
      Control, London 1979.

3 The structure of the office labour force

Many of the characteristics of the journey to work are a direct result of the structure of the labour force and this chapter will be used, firstly, to compare the recruiting activity of the offices which have moved to each centre using evidence provided by the management interviews and from the questionnaires completed by individual office workers, and secondly, to consider briefly whether there are significant changes in office recruitment at decentralized locations over time and whether there are important differences between centres, perhaps as a result of location differences. Trends in staff recruitment can also be expected to affect the demand for housing in and around the reception centres and this chapter therefore provides some introductory material which will be helpful when considering the contents of Chapter 4 which examines some aspects of the demand for housing by office staff.

The majority of the offices completed their relocations to the study towns after 1970. [1] Moves by large offices such as 93 (1975) and 90 (1974) to Reading; 94 (1967) and 85 (1973) to Swindon; and 66 (1970) and 67 (1974) to Southampton are typical of this trend. Some offices had, however, moved from central London as far back as 1964 and had therefore had plenty of time to become well assimilated into local labour markets. Indeed, in all the centres most of the companies which relocated prior to 1970 had completed this activity by 1969 or 1968 after which time there is often a gap of some years before later movers arrive in 1972 or 1973, as at Watford, Swindon and Liverpool.

COMPANY INFORMATION ON RECRUITMENT

Respondents were asked at the management interview if they could provide an indication of the number of central London employees who had transferred to the new location by the time the company had completed its relocation programme. Because of the large time lags and the lack of familiarity with circumstances in the mid-1960's in some cases respondents were unable to provide any figures but from the evidence provided by two-thirds (26) of the sample it is clear that the likelihood of being able to retain central London staff continues to be dependent on the distance moved by their employers. [2] Out of a total labour force of 787 employees at Watford in 1976 only 17 were formerly employed in the central London offices of the organisations concerned.[3] This is much lower than the figure of one-third (419/1231) recorded in the Economic Consultants survey which also mentions that the offices had little difficulty in obtaining staff.[4] In Reading where only two small companies did not provide data, almost 600 out of an establishment of 3157 employees had moved from central London with their employers and this is more in accord with expectations. Although Swindon is further from London than Reading over 1,000 central London recruits are estimated to have moved there with their companies out of a 1976 total establishment of 4501.[5] This provides some indication that the availability of housing in Swindon, particularly for junior office staff, may be an invaluable inducement for migrants who are not otherwise expected to move such long distances with their London employers. The proportion of central London staff is much the same at Southampton, although the absolute figure which this represents is much lower than for Swindon, with some 260 out of 905 employees in this category. The absorption of the demand for housing in the Southampton area with its much larger population and range of residential areas within easy travelling distance should not present difficulties if the size of companies decentralizing to this area continues to be in the small to medium size range. Liverpool conforms with the expectation of a low number of central London movers with just 47 in this group out of an establishment of 982 employees in the four companies. There is, therefore, some evidence of distance decay in the propensity of central London workers to move with their employers but it is also the case that other variables, particularly housing availability, can be expected to modify the general form of the relationship.

On the basis of the statistics for local recruitment from the survey towns and their immediate vicinity it cannot be assumed that shortfalls in the number of employees prepared to transfer with their employers from central London will be made up from the local labour pool. This only appears to be the case at Liverpool where most of the office staff (821/982) have been recruited from local sources but in Reading (716/3157) and Swindon (596/4501) this has certainly not happened. The analysis of data relating to the previous place of residence of respondents to the employee questionnaire (discussed in Chapter 4) provides a clue to these low figures. Many of the large offices in this survey have used decentralization as a 'centralization' exercise whereby staff are brought together from diverse locations elsewhere in the country or, in one instance (office 90, Reading) from overseas. Therefore the size of the decentralizing organisation, the spatial disposition of other parts of its activities and the status of the decentralized establishment in the organisational hierarchy may well reduce the demand for recruits from local sources to levels considerably below expectations. Since most large enterprises will almost certainly have establishments elsewhere it is likely that moves of this kind will have proportionally less effect on locally based demand for office workers than smaller and less complex organisations.

EMPLOYEE SURVEY INFORMATION ON RECRUITMENT

It is encouraging to find that the pattern of response from employees in the questionnaire survey conforms quite closely with the statistics provided by employers (Fig. 3.1). The importance of central London recruits in the samples for Reading and Swindon, especially for male office staff, is very clear with 35-55 percent in this category. The offices in these two centres have employed rather fewer local recruits than those at Watford, Southampton and Liverpool where this group comprise 35-45 percent of the labour force. Staff recruited from locations other than central London or the local area by their present employers comprise a significant share of the sample in Watford (15 percent) and Southampton (10 percent) and these figures are further inflated by employees who have transferred from other employers, especially at Watford. There is an important dichotomy, evident in Fig. 3.1, between male and female recruits. Local recruitment is largely satisfied by the latter, including office workers entering full-time work for the first time or re-entering the job market after several months or years absence. The majority of female recruits transfer from other local employers, perhaps attracted by the higher wage rates used by some decentralizing firms to attract personnel. They also comprise well over 60-70 percent of the respondents who defined themselves as 'not previously employed'. The imbalance between males and females is indicated by the values of the contingency coefficient (C) for the relationship between place of previous employment and sex. The values range between 0.38 (Watford) and 0.49 (Liverpool) and although it is not possible to attach statistical significance to C it provides a useful indication of the strength of association between two variables in a contingency table.[6]

Because of the large proportion of central London recruits in the Reading and Swindon samples the relationship between distance of each town from London and the number of mobile staff is distorted and is certainly not as clearly demonstrated as in the Follow-Up Survey. It is, however, rather better illustrated by central London recruits who have taken up employment in the study towns after working for other employers in London.

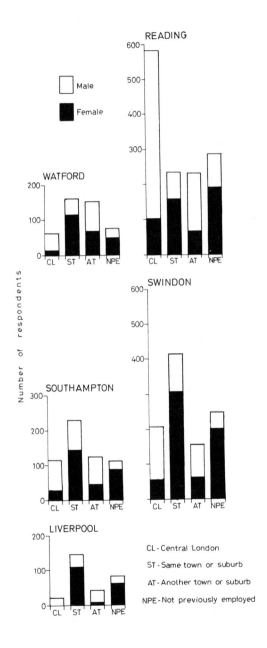

Figure 3.1 The structure of the office labour force by
place of recruitment

The overall distribution of recruits by previous workplace
in all five centres can be used to calculate the expected
number of recruits in each group in each centre to
see whether there are large discrepancies between
observed and expected patterns. On this basis, central
London recruits are only over-represented by a large
margin (585/358) in Reading and are under-represented
elsewhere, especially in Liverpool. There are more
local recruits, than would be expected from the overall
pattern of response, in all the centres except Reading
with the largest excess in Swindon. Recruits from
other locations are represented at a higher level
than expected in Watford (almost 50 percent more than
predicted) and Southampton where the difference is
more marginal. Only the Swindon and Liverpool samples
comprise more previously unemployed recruits than
expected. The Reading decentralized offices are particularly notable in that as well as importing large numbers
of central London staff, they have also recruited
almost as many previously unemployed as expected (288/297).
These contrasts in recruitment by the offices in each
centre are worth noting since they are likely to moderate
or exaggerate some of the attributes of the journey
to work patterns to be discussed later.

There is an even better association between sex
and occupation status of office recruits in all five
centres (Fig. 3.2). The values of C range between
0.48 and 0.57 and reflect the predominant demand for
female clerical workers who account for 75 percent
of the females in the sample. Male clerical workers
are much less significant and the majority of male
respondents, in contrast to the Follow-Up Survey,
are in managerial or supervisory occupations; only
the offices in Southampton have less than 40 percent
of the male respondents in managerial posts. For
all five towns, therefore, 22 percent of the respondents
are in managerial positions and this can also be expected
to exert considerable influence on journey to work
behaviour; the equivalent figure in the Follow-Up
Survey was 11 percent. Dispersed government offices
are not well represented in the cluster survey so
that clerical workers are probably under-represented
when compared with the working population as a whole
while the tendency for the offices which have moved
to Reading and Swindon to bring large numbers of their
former central London staff increases the likelihood
of managerial or professional posts occurring in the
sample. Clerical workers are less likely to move
with their employers than employees in higher level
occupations.[7]

Over 70 percent of the managers in Reading formerly
worked in central London but in the other centres,
where the total number of managers is much lower,

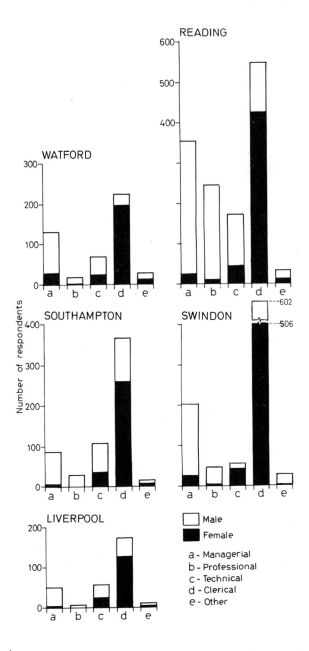

Figure 3.2 Occupation structure of the office labour
force

Table 3.1

Selected aspects of employee recruitment at offices in survey towns

Survey Town	Previous Workplace	Occupation status					c^1	% Female	Age (%) Under 21	Over 45
		Managerial	Professional	Sup/Tech	Clerical	Other				
Watford	Central London	25.2	26.3	12.8	8.1	7.4		23.4	1.6	47.5
	Same town	22.8	21.1	27.1	43.2	65.4		71.8	10.2	39.5
	Elsewhere	43.9	36.9	37.2	28.4	15.3	0.39	45.2	8.0	34.0
	NPE²	8.1	15.8	22.9	20.3	11.5		64.9	24.0	8.0
	N =	(123)	(19)	(90)	(222)	(26)				
	% over 45	43.5	26.3	22.4	27.8	67.9				
Reading	Central London	73.3	50.0	53.8	18.6	15.2		17.3	2.9	37.1
	Same town	7.1	7.1	17.8	27.4	51.5		67.2	14.8	5.7
	Elsewhere	18.3	29.6	16.0	11.3	24.2	0.52	28.8	23.0	11.5
	NPE	1.4	13.3	12.4	41.6	9.1		66.3	59.2	4.6
	N =	(355)	(240)	(169)	(539)	(33)				
	% over 45	42.2	15.3	28.9	14.0	58.1				
Swindon	Central London	51.8	32.7	19.2	8.9	7.7		22.5	2.9	35.7
	Same town	23.3	32.7	38.5	44.5	46.2		73.9	20.2	20.0
	Elsewhere	22.3	24.4	21.4	11.0	10.3	0.74	44.0	5.9	20.8
	NPE	2.5	10.2	20.9	35.6	35.9		77.4	60.7	8.8
	N =	(193)	(44)	(144)	(607)	(39)				
	% over 45	36.3	15.6	30.0	13.9	52.2				

/Continued ......

43

Table 3.1 (Continued)

Survey Town	Previous Workplace	Occupation status					C[1]	Female	Age (%)	
		Managerial	Professional	Sup/Tech	Clerical	Other			Under 21	Over 45
Southampton	Central London	48.7	53.3	29.0	7.2	6.7		23.5	0.9	40.5
	Same town	23.7	10.0	37.0	46.9	33.3		62.2	14.8	34.1
	Elsewhere	25.0	36.7	26.0	18.9	20.0	0.49	35.2	3.2	35.2
	NPE	2.5	-	8.0	26.9	40.0		77.9	34.3	22.9
	N =	(80)	(30)	(100)	(360)	(15)				
	% over 45	55.3	24.1	35.9	29.1	60.0				
Liverpool	Central London	26.6	20.0	8.8	1.8	10.0		0.0	0.0	40.9
	Same town	22.3	20.0	40.3	62.5	30.0		74.1	18.2	27.7
	Elsewhere	40.0	20.0	17.5	6.4	10.0	0.52	21.9	9.8	12.2
	NPE	11.1	40.0	33.3	29.2	50.0		74.4	23.3	21.9
	N =	(45)	(5)	(57)	(171)	(10)				
	% over 45	35.4	25.0	22.4	21.3	30.0				

Note: 1. Contingency coefficient.
2. Not previously employed.

Source: Office Survey, 1976.

44

it is just as likely that these employees will be brought in from elsewhere (Table 3.1). Central London also acts as an important source for professional staff in the Reading, Swindon and Southampton offices and, in general, less than 20 percent of the employees in this group have been attracted from local sources. The majority of clerical workers have previously worked locally or have entered employment for the first time; in Reading over 41 percent of the clerical recruits are in this category and 36 percent in Swindon. The values of C (see Table 3.1) confirm, therefore, that there is a clear association between occupation status and previous workplace of uecentralized office staff. The table also shows that the majority of local recruits are females who are most likely not to be represented amongst the central London group. Given these differences, there are also clear distinction in the age structure of recruits (Table 3.1). Most central London recruits are over 45 and will have very different housing, education and other requirements to the younger office staff who are more likely to be local recruits and often previously unemployed. Hence, for example, 35-45 percent of the employees in managerial occupations are over 45 compared with only 20-25 percent of the clerical workers.

Using the same procedure for comparing observed with expected distributions of occupation groups in each town, it emerges that managers are over-represented in Watford (131/102) and Reading (357/292) but not elsewhere. Professionals are also over-represented by a considerable margin in Reading (244/123) but grossly under-represented in the other centres. Thus, both Watford and Reading are deficient in clerical occupations while Swindon and Southampton have the largest excesses; 606/538 and 369/306 respectively. There are therefore two centres with offices which are oriented towards higher order office occupations, Watford and Reading, and three in which the offices are dominated by supervisory, clerical and other office jobs.

STAFF RECRUITMENT THROUGH TIME

Office employees were asked to indicate the month and year in which they started their jobs at the decentralized offices and the distribution of the returns for 1965-76 is illustrated in Fig. 3.3 according to their previous place of employment. The bar graphs for each year show the absolute number of recruits in that year sub-divided according to location of previous workplace. In all five centres demand shows a sharp increase during the early 1970's, especially in Reading and Swindon, following the decentralization

45

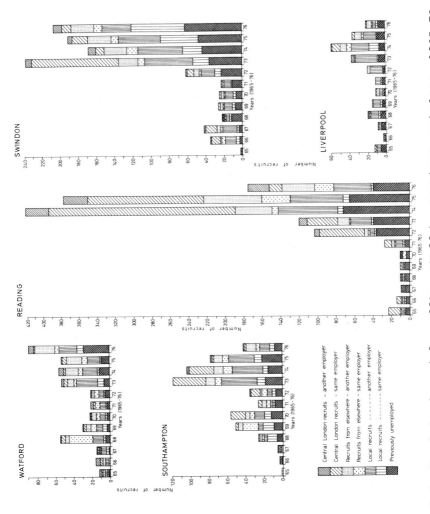

Figure 3.3   Absolute demand for office staff by previous workplace, 1965-76

activity which took place some 2-3 years prior to the survey in 1976. A second but much lower peak occurs in most centres between 1967 and 1969 when decentralization was increasing its momentum because of the severe shortage of office space in central London caused by the office development permit controls.[8] Perhaps the most significant feature of the demand for office workers represented in Fig. 3.3 is that during periods of high activity, such as 1974 and 1975 in Reading or 1973 and 1974 in Southampton and Swindon, the contribution of local recruits and the previously unemployed to meeting this demand is proportionately lower than during other more stable periods. Certainly the absolute number of local recruits expands as demand is triggered by incoming offices but the expansion is not as large as would be expected from the overall change in demand. The best examples of this are provided by Reading and Swindon where, for the former, the overall demand tripled from 1973 to 1974 but only just doubled for the previously unemployed and local recruits and for the latter overall demand increased four times between 1972 and 1973 but only doubled for local recruits during the same period.

A similar, but perhaps less exaggerated, pattern also occurs in the three other centres and it suggests that because decentralizing firms bring central London or other recruits with them, reception towns should perhaps expect a retardation of short term demand for local labour but should also anticipate a lagged effect of the kind well illustrated at Southampton, Swindon and Reading. In other words, the share of demand which will be satisfied by the local supply of office labour will increase some 2-3 years after offices have become established when the impetus for attracting central London staff has gone and, apart from bringing in office staff from other parts of the country, employers must increasingly depend on local sources. The only problem here, however, is that the number of staff required also seems to fall off sharply so that in absolute terms the number of jobs created or requiring to be filled because of staff turnover is much lower than during the 12-18 months before and after relocation takes place. Southampton, Liverpool and Reading show this well while Swindon is somewhat unusual with a revival of demand in 1975 and 1976 which is increasingly dependent on local recruits.

PART TIME WORK AND FLEXIBLE HOURS

One attraction of office work for potential female recruits is the possibility of part-time work which allows domestic commitments to be more easily accommodated.[9] Some 40 percent of all female employees in

Table 3.2

Full-time and part-time employment by sex - offices in survey towns

Type of Employment	Survey towns										Overall Total		Follow-Up Survey
	Watford M	F	Reading M	F	Swindon M	F	Southampton M	F	Liverpool M	F			
Full-time	94.4	71.6	99.6	93.8	99.3	93.5	100.0	94.5	100.0	87.2	3644	95.4	(97.5)
Part-time (10-30 hrs)	3.2	26.8	0.2	5.9	0.5	5.7	-	4.5	-	11.7	168	4.4	(2.5)
Part-time (LT 10 hrs)	0.9	-	-	0.4	-	0.2	-	0.3	-	1.1	8	0.2	
Total	216[2]	261	837	528	432	644	304	309	119	180	3820	100	(100)
	(100)[2]	(100)	(100)	(100)	(100)	(100)	(100)	(100)	(100)	(100)			
C^1	0.31		0.18		0.14		0.17		0.23				

Notes: 1. Contingency coefficient.
        2. Some percentages will not sum to 100 because of non-response.

Sources: Office Survey 1976.
         Follow-Up Survey 1976.

Table 3.3
Use of flexible working hours in survey offices
- by sex

| Survey Town | | Flexible hours | | Proportion of total |
		Yes	No	in each town
Watford	Males	32 (14.8)[1]	184	3.5
	Females	29 (11.1)	232	3.3
Reading	Males	734 (87.7)	103	79.7
	Females	437 (82.8)	91	49.1
Swindon	Males	49 (11.3)	383	5.3
	Females	256 (39.8)	388	28.8
Southampton	Males	77 (25.3)	224	8.4
	Females	131 (42.4)	178	14.7
Liverpool	Males	29 (24.4)	90	3.1
	Females	37 (20.6)	143	4.2
Totals	Males	921 (68.1)	984	100
	Females	890 (55.9)	1032	100

Note: 1. Proportion of males and females on
           flexible hours in each centre.

Source: Office Survey, 1976.

Great Britain were part-time workers in 1976 compared with just 28 percent in 1968.[10] The equivalent figures for male workers are 5 percent and 2 percent respectively. Apart from Watford and Liverpool, part-time employment does not account for a significant proportion of the respondents and amounts to approximately 6 percent of all females in the three other centres (Table 3.2). The majority of part-time staff work 10-30 hours a week; almost 27 percent of the female respondents in Watford are employed on this basis and almost 12 percent in Liverpool. The information on part-time employment in these two centres will be considered again later in relation to other variables such as travel mode and trip time for the journey to work since part-time workers are unlikely to be able to travel as far to work as full-time workers.

In addition to the opportunities for part-time work provided by white collar occupations, the possibility of working flexible hours, first introduced in Britain in 1971, can also be an attractive feature for existing and potential recruits.[11] Flexible hours provide an opportunity for avoiding the work transport congestion associated with peak hour travel, so reducing costs to individuals and commuters at large but relatively little is known about their actual effect on journey to work behaviour.[12] The incidence of flexible hours in offices still varies considerably, however, and Reading is the only centre where more than 75 percent of the respondents participate in flexible working hours (Table 3.3). In Southampton over 40 percent of the female respondents are on flexible hours but only 25 percent of males. A similar dichotomy occurs at Swindon with 40 and 11 percent respectively. Flexible hours are generally voluntary and are not necessarily an attractive alternative to conventional working hours for all employees but are certainly more attractive, on the evidence available here, to female office workers. Almost half of all the employees on flexible hours are in Reading, followed by Swindon and Southampton. Apart from female office staff at Southampton and Swindon the number at the other centres is very low. There are rather more employees on flexible hours than was revealed in the Follow-Up offices. The larger share of recent movers in the present survey probably accounts for the difference because relocation and recruitment policies come under close scrutiny at such times and flexible hours have only relatively recently become widely known and accepted.

In the two centres where the majority of office staff are on flexible hours, there are only minor distinctions between the proportion of each occupation group who participate (Table 3.4). The variations are much greater in Watford and Southampton because

Table 3.4

Occupation status and flexible hours - offices in survey towns

Occupation status	Proportion of each occupation group on flexible hours					
	Watford	Reading	Swindon	Southampton	Liverpool	Total
Managerial	17.6 (23)[1]	82.2 (295)	8.8 (17)	31.0 (27)	6.0 (3)	44.7 (365)
Professional	47.4 (9)	87.7 (214)	10.2 (5)	3.3 (1)	40.0 (2)	66.6 (231)
Sup/Tech	8.3 (5)	86.0 (147)	26.4 (48)	41.1 (44)	50.0 (29)	46.7 (273)
Clerical	38.3 (23)	86.2 (474)	38.7 (235)	65.2 (135)	16.3 (28)	46.7 (895)
Other	- (-)	100.0 (33)	- (-)	- (-)	20.0 (2)	29.2 (35)
Overall Prop.	12.5 (60)	85.7(1163)	28.5 (305)	33.7 (207)	21.7 (64)	63.0(2390)

Note: 1.   Absolute number of trips represented by the proportion
              of respondents in each occupation group on flexible
              hours.

Source: Office Survey, 1976.

51

of the lower adoption rate by the respondent offices
and the differences in their organisational structure.
Hence, the fact that 47 percent of professional staff
in the Watford sample are on flexible hours does not
mean that they are more amenable to them but that
their employers happen to have given them the choice.
In Southampton, clerical workers comprise a large
part of the sample and are therefore more likely to
be participating but the difficulty of making generalisa-
tions is stressed by the equivalent figure for clerical
workers in Liverpool (see Table 3.4). Overall therefore
it seems that managerial and professional office workers
are just as likely to work flexible hours as clerical
workers.

In common with the Follow-Up Survey it is clear
that all office departments are not able to operate
on the basis of flexible hours. During the interviews
with management representatives it was suggested that
this can cause resentment between employees but respondents were mostly of the view that flexible hours
offer more advantages than disadvantages for individuals
and their employers. Flexible hours are used to enhance
employee/company relations, with a view to improving
efficiency and to reduce overtime costs. As was noted
in the Follow-Up Survey, the journey to work advantages
for individual office staff are not paramount in the
management decision to adopt flexible working hours
but most employers did recognise the opportunities
provided for making the journey to work easier. The
principal disadvantages of flexible hours mentioned
by employers were largely concerned with the excessive
duration of the core period and the difficulty of
carrying over time saved beyond pre-defined cut-off
points. This could be alleviated by moving the end
of core time back to 3 p.m. rather than 4 p.m. which
is the normal cut-off point. One company also suggested
that the flexibility of the system presents problems
of coupling the work activity of those office staff
who follow regular hours of work with those who never
start or finish at the same time each day. In cases
where deadlines are in operation employees are entitled
to leave their desks whether or not the operation
has been completed and this makes business objectives
more difficult to achieve.

NOTES AND REFERENCES

(1)   Year of move of each office to present address as
      follows:

      Watford: 1965 (1), 1966 (1), 1968 (1), 1973 (3),
                   1974 (1).

      Reading: 1965 (2), 1966 (2), 1971 (3), 1972 (1),
                   1973 (1), 1974 (1), 1975 (1).

Swindon: 1966 (1), 1967 (1), 1971 (2), 1973 (2).

Southampton: 1964 (1), 1968 (1), 1969 (1), 1970 (1), 1972 (1), 1973 (1), 1974 (1).

Liverpool: 1965 (1), 1967 (1), 1974 (1), 1975 (1).

(2) Examples are given in E. Hammond, London to Durham: A Study of the Transfer of the Post Office Savings Certificate Division, Rowntree Research Unit, Durham 1968; M. Bateman et.al., Office Staff on the Move, Location of Offices Bureau, Research Paper No. 6, London 1971; E. Sidwell, 'London to Bristol: The experience of a major office organisation and to staff', in P.W. Daniels (ed.), Spatial Patterns of Office Growth and Location, Wiley, London 1979, pp. 349-72; M. Bateman and D. Burtenshaw, Office Decentraliza-tion to a Provincial Centre, Social Science Research Council (Final Report) London 1976; P.W. Daniels, op.cit., 1972; P.W. Daniels, A Follow-Up Study of the Journey to Work at Decentralized Offices in Britain: Final Report (Part I), Departments of Environment and Transport, London 1978.

(3) To some extent this understates the true proportion since your offices were unable to provide data in response to this question.

(4) Location of Offices Bureau, Demand and Supply for Office Workers and the Local Impact of Office Development. A Report prepared by Economic Consultants Ltd., Location of Offices Bureau, London 1971, p. 75.

(5) The term 'recruits' is used to refer to employees moving with their employers from central London as well as to office workers recruited from other employers in the same area.

(6) Pearson's cortingency coefficient (C) is a measure of association based on chi-square (X^2) where:

$$C = \frac{X^2}{X^2 + N}$$

The value of C becomes '0' when the variables are independent and the upper limit for a 2 x 2 table is 0.707. This upper limit increases as the number of rows and columns in the contin-gency table increases but it is always less than 1.0. Hence C is difficult to interpret as accurately as Pearson's correlation coefficient or Spearman's rank coefficient. See for example, H.M. Blalock, Social Statistics, McGraw Hill, New York 1960.

(7)   See for example E. Hammond, op.cit.; M. Bateman
        et.al., op.cit.

(8)   For a more detailed discussion see P.W. Daniels,
        Office Location: An Urban and Regional Study,
        Bell, London 1975, pp. 170-72; R. Barras, 'The
        returns from office development and investment',
        Working Note 514, Centre for Environmental
        Studies, London 1978.

(9)   Some interesting statistics on the growth and
        future trends in the level of male and female
        part-time employment in the tertiary sector
        are included in J. Marquand, The Role of the
        Tertiary Sector in Regional Policy: U.K. Report
        (Draft), Centre for Environmental Studies and
        the University of Louvain-la-Neuve, London
        1978, pp. 34-38. The tertiary sector contains
        more part-time workers of both sexes and the
        proportion has been growing more rapidly than
        in the manufacturing sector.

(10)   See statistics given in Department of Employment
        Gazette, Vol. 85, 1977.

(11)   P.J. Sloane, 'Changing patterns of working hours',
        Manpower Paper No. 13, Her Majesty's Stationery
        Office, London 1975; J. Bolton, Flexible Working
        Hours, Anbar Publications, London 1972; S.
        Rousham, Flexible Working Hours Today: Practices
        and Experiences in over Fifty British Organisations,
        British Institute of Management, London 1973;
        P. Erg and K.G. McLean, 'Variable work hours:
        who benefits?', Traffic Engineering, Vol. 16,
        1975, pp. 17-25.

(12)   P.W. Daniels, 'Flexible hours and the journey
        to work to office establishments', paper recently
        submitted to Transportation Planning and Technology,
        Loughborough 1979.

4 Some aspects of the demand for housing

The relocation of office functions invariably involves transfer and recruitment of staff both from within and outside an organisation and this inevitably generates changes in place of residence for at least some of the office workers. The volume of change is directly related to the distance moved by an office. There have been several studies which have considered this aspect of office relocation but most of them have been based on case studies of single office establishments which have moved to Ipswich, Portsmouth, Ashford, Bristol or Durham.[1] Such studies have permitted quite detailed questions about the structural aspects of demand for housing by relocated office workers, and the way that these are satisfied in reception areas, to be considered in some depth. In addition, the wider social impact of decentralization on office migrants has also been considered and summarised in a recent paper by Bateman and Burtenshaw.[2] It is not the intention here to add to this literature, rather an attempt is made to consider some of the spatial aspects of the demand for housing in and around the towns included in this survey. A time dimension has also been introduced into the analysis in an attempt to show that in-migrant organisations which may expand or contract their staff requirements in the way already illustrated in Fig. 3.3 have long term effects on local housing markets. Both these aspects of residential relocation by office workers have been largely neglected in previous studies. In addition, there is also scope in this study for making comments on a comparison of data from several offices in different urban areas rather than relying on the results from one case study.

Before disaggregating the data it is worth noting that the levels of residential mobility shown by male and female decentralized office staff who have made at least one residential change immediately prior to or shortly after changing their place of employment are very uniform for each centre (Table 4.1). Approximately 55 per cent of all male respondents in each centre have changed address at least once; female office staff tend to be less mobile with approximately 35 percent classified as movers. Overall, about 48 percent of the respondents are from households which have moved at least once, although there is clearly no indication in the table as to the proportion of these moves which were entirely caused by the relocation decisions of decentralized offices or as by-products of accepting a new job with a decentralized employer.

55

Table 4.1

Proportion of office employees involved in at least one residential change

Sex	Watford 1		Reading		Survey towns Swindon		Southampton		Liverpool		Total	
	Movers	%	Movers	%	Movers	%	Movers	%	Movers	%	Movers	%
Males	114	52.8	430	51.4	263	60.9	168	55.3	66	55.5	1041	56.1
Females	82	31.4	192	36.4	207	32.1	132	42.7	71	39.4	755	40.2
Total	196	41.1	622	45.6	470	44.5	300	48.9	137	45.8	1796	48.1
c^2	0.21		0.14		0.27		0.12		0.15			

Notes: 1. Percentage of all male respondents

2. Contingency coefficient.

Source: Office Survey, 1976.

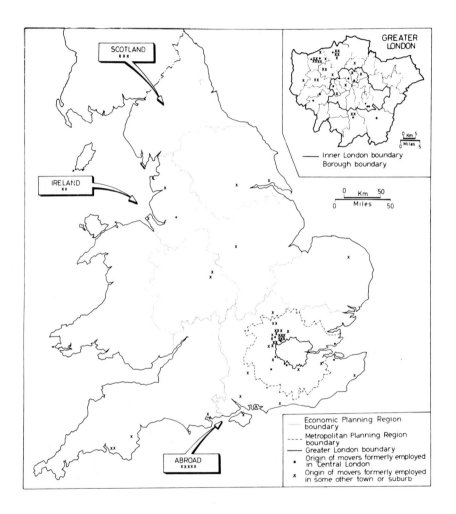

Figure 4.1   Previous residences   of Watford migrants

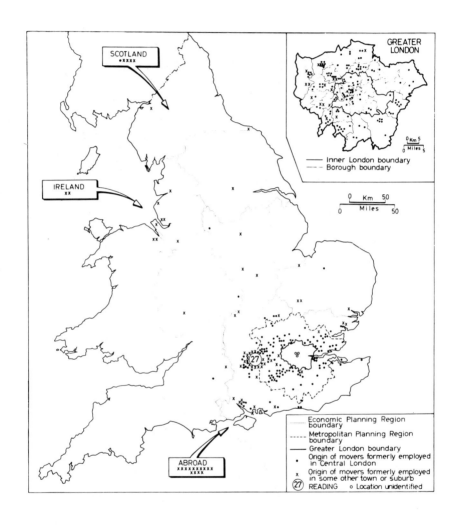

Figure 4.2   Previous residences of Reading migrants

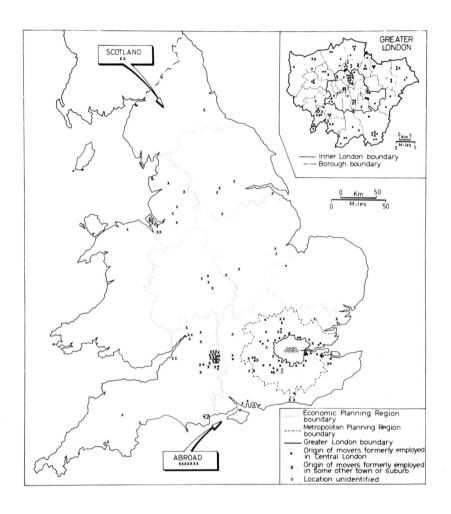

Figure 4.3   Previous residences of Swindon migrants

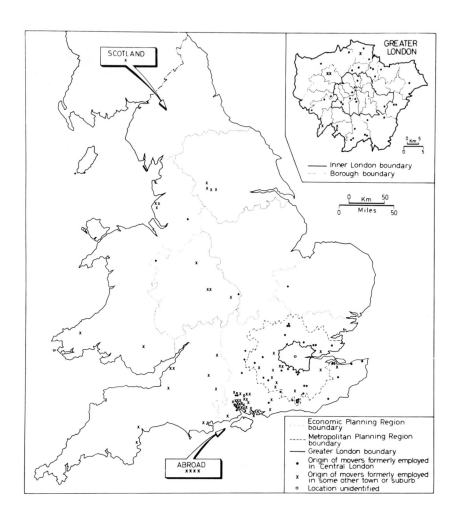

Figure 4.4   Previous residences of Southampton migrants

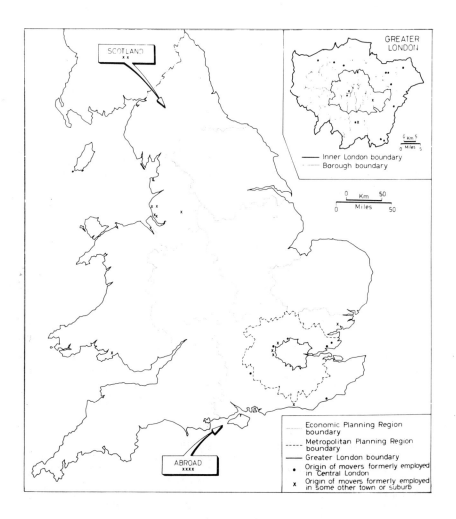

Figure 4.5   Previous residences of Liverpool migrants

The values of C shown in Table 4.1 indicate that the
sex of respondents only provides a moderate indication
of residential mobility and other factors such as
previous workplace or occupation of spouse (for female
office staff) are more likely to be important influences
on this characteristic.

AREAS OF ORIGIN OF MIGRANT HOUSEHOLDS

The location of the previous residences of office
staff (excluding local recruits who have changed address)
are shown in a series of maps (Figs. 4.1 - 4.5).
The maps are derived from the addresses of respondents
immediately prior to taking up their jobs in the decentralized offices and who have subsequently changed
their address.   Each map gives the information provided
by office workers in each study centre and shows the
distribution of previous residences within the framework
of the Economic Planning Regions, outside the South
East, and for smaller sub-divisions within the South
East Region.   It can be expected that the majority
of central London recruits will move from the Greater
London (G.L.C.) and the Outer Metropolitan Area (O.M.A.)
while the pattern for staff recruited from elsewhere
will be more diffuse and will to some extent be a
product of corporate factors such as the location
of other establishments within the same company or
of recruitment policies.

   The aggregated figures show that over 50 percent
of the migrant central London recruits previously
lived within the G.L.C. and one-third of these lived
in Inner London.   A further 27 percent previously
lived in the O.M.A. and the remainder in the Outer
South East (O.S.E.) or, in some cases, beyond.   Only
17 percent of the migrants classified as recruits
from other locations previously resided in Greater
London and only 12 percent of them moved from Inner
London.   Almost 70 percent of the recruits from elsewhere
who have had to change address have come from outside
the Metropolitan Area as the maps clearly show.   Office
decentralization therefore generates a complex pattern
of "predictable" residential migration over similar
distances and a set of longer distance movements which
are far more difficult to forecast because of their
spatial diversity and the variable contributory factors
involved.   Some may be the result of company staffing
policies while others may arise from decisions by
individuals to seek employment in a different part
of the country.

The origins of Watford migrants (Fig. 4.1) show a surprising bias to locations which are proximal to the town, such as adjacent areas of Hertfordshire and the north western boroughs of the G.L.C. It is usually the case that residential change will only take place when dependence on the existing place of residence creates unacceptable conditions for the journey to work so that in Watford's case, for example, it would only seem likely that office staff who need to travel across London would find it necessary to change address. It seems, however, that many offices in Watford have moved in the direction from which their staff already travelled to work in central London so that the need to make residential changes has been minimised. The large number of recruits from elsewhere who are within easy travelling distance (on the basis of the distribution shown in Fig. 4.1) have therefore been the principal source of demand for housing in the Watford area but, as a later section on the destinations of migrant households will show, these employees have not been moving nearer to Watford in order to minimise travel distances but reveal a tendency to move further away.

The pattern for Reading migrants is dominated by movers from the G.L.C. and the remainder of the Metropolitan Area (Fig. 4.2). The previous residential distribution of central London recruits is a broad reflection of the overall pattern of commuting into central London but with a bias towards Outer London and the O.M.A. Some 33 percent of the migrant households have moved from Greater London with 25 percent previously resident in Inner London. The eastern areas of Inner London and the boroughs of the Outer North East sector of the G.L.C. are the only areas from which there have been relatively few migrants and both areas are not prime sources of office labour for central London. The few recruits from employers elsewhere in Greater London have moved from the western side of the city from which Reading is moderately accessible, particularly by train. Indeed, there is a 'corridor' of low residential mobility from central London through Hounslow and beyond to Reading which suggests that employees along this route have found it less necessary to change place of residence. The 'corridor' was also previously used by 27 staff who lived in Reading and travelled to work in central London and who have subsequently changed address. A number of offices in Reading (e.g. the large office 84) did mention that several of their employees already lived in the area when the decision was made to decentralize.

The Swindon sample also contains a large number of migrants who previously worked in central London but a larger number of their residential changes have emanated from areas within Greater London than is the case at Reading (Fig. 4.3). Almost 60 percent of the central London recruits have moved from the G.L.C. which is some 10 percent above the average for all five centres. · The dominance of locations in the outer suburbs, typical of Reading migrants, is also lower; approximately 36 percent of the movers have left the northern and western parts of Inner London. In common with Reading, the majority of movers comprise a residential pattern which reflects the extensive labour catchment area of central London offices but it also includes employees living within easy reach of Swindon (several of whom previously travelled to central London) who have probably moved house for reasons other than those connected with the journey to work. The previous addresses of migrants previously employed elsewhere show a wide and variable distribution similar to the Reading group but with the added element of some locational specificity in the origin of movers. This is a good example of organisational factors imposing some order on the pattern of residential change with two of the Swindon offices having notable company activities in the Wirral/north Cheshire and in the Birmingham area respectively. All these migrant households are those of employees in the two companies who have been transferred to the Swindon offices. Decentralization of large offices which are part of multi-site organisations can therefore generate changes in housing supply in areas far removed from the Metropolitan Area, where the largest changes in supply are likely to occur and where the cumulative impact on housing supply may be less apparent than in some of the smaller urban areas which are affected in other parts of the country.

The origins of migrant office staff in Southampton who previously worked in centres other than central London or the local area also reveal a dichotomous distribution of the kind which occurs at Watford (Fig. 4.4). Even though many of this group live within travelling distance of Southampton they have still elected to change address. It may be that they are less tolerant of any minor deterioration in their travel to work conditions because they are already conditioned to think in terms of short distance journeys and times and are therefore more prepared to make short distance residential changes in order to restore equilibrium. For central London recruits the prospect of a shorter journey to work is attractive if they are able to move house but in some cases the prospect of long reverse commuting trips which may only represent marginal time savings but virtually no overcrowding or traffic delays may be considered an acceptable alternative and will discourage residential changes and all that they imply for the households involved.

Less than 70 percent of the central London recruits at Southampton have moved in response to decentralization and of these only 40 percent have left the G.L.C. (28 percent from Inner London). But the equivalent figures for Watford, Reading and Swindon; 50 percent, 51.5 percent and 32.5 percent respectively are much lower than can be explained by the distance decay rule which would lead us to expect that at least as many central London recruits would change address as a result of decentralization to Swindon as have changed address in the Southampton case. The opportunies for reverse commuting and directional bias in office decentralization caused by the residential distribution of employees prior to relocation clearly distorts the basic generalisation which is usually made about distance decay. It seems therefore, that if offices move to centres further from London it cannot be assumed that they will generate a larger demand for housing in and around the area in proportion to the number of central London recruits or staff recruited from elsewhere.

Almost all the movers at the Liverpool offices came from London and the South East but they only comprise 7.5 percent of the total responaents and, therefore, do not represent a significant demand for housing in the Merseyside area (Fig. 4.4). All the central London recruits had to change address which accords with expectations and suggests that decentralization to locations within and adjacent to the South East probably provides more residential flexibility (in association with a superior transport network) for office workers than the distances involved would suggest. Beyond a certain distance threshold, not identifiable here, and often taking account of transport networks it becomes imperative for office workers to change address or, alternatively, to seek some other location at which to work.

Data on the origins of migrants provides a general indication of the effect of office relocation on the release of housing in the Metropolitan Area but it does not indicate the type of accommodation vacated, or its value. This also affects the kind of accommodation sought by migrating households at the receiving locations but this aspect, which has been considered by Hammond or Bateman and Burtenshaw for example, is not within the terms of reference of this study.[3]

Once the decision has been made by a household to seek a new address the search area can be extensive and the demand for housing is unlikely to be entirely focused on accommodation within the reception centre.[4] In the particular context of office relocation this has been well illustrated by Bateman et. al. who have

shown that the search areas for housing reflect individual
aspirations and perceptions of the availability and
environmental attributes of housing in areas which
are usually very different to those from which they
are moving.[2] London recruits are particularly interesting
in this respect and for many of them the opportunity
to move out of the conurbation and its environs provides
an opportunity, at least in theory, to adopt 'anti-
urban' life styles in a low density rural environment.
The ability to achieve individual objectives is dependent
on income and the value of assets being disposed of
in the areas from which migrants are moving but it
seems that migrants who anticipate 'savings' as a
result of leaving high cost residential suburbs in
London for lower cost areas elsewhere are not likely
to achieve them because they tend to purchase additional
space over and above what they may really need with
the result that their housing costs return to the
levels prevalent in the areas from which they have
moved.[6]

It had been originally intended that some of these
issues would be examined in the present study by undertaking in-depth interviews with a target sample of
migrant households, particularly from the London area.
Provision was indeed made in the employee questionnaire
(see Appendix) for respondents to indicate whether
they would be prepared to participate in an extended
interview, if required, at a later date. In order
to retain their anonymity (they were asked to give
their names) in relation to the information already
provided in the questionnaire it was arranged for
their response to this question to be detached from
the pro-forma and retained by their employers. Inter-
viewees could subsequently be identified by a code
number printed on the tear-off slip and the main part
of the questionnaire. Unfortunately, the volume of
work subsequently connected with questionnaire processing
and data capture did not leave enough time or resources
for the proposed interviews to be undertaken and a
useful opportunity to monitor the motivations, aspirations
and successes of migrant office workers in relation
to housing and the journey to work, in particular,
has been missed. The response from office workers
who completed the questionnaires and assistance provided
by employers does suggest, however, that future research
workers who want to adopt a two stage approach to
the study of residential relocation as a result of
employment decentralization would not be confronted
by lack of support from participants.[7]

WATFORD

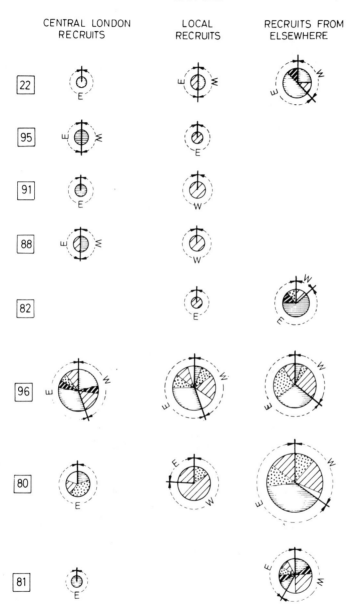

Figure 4.6   Initial residential location choice by relocating households, Watford offices

READING

CENTRAL LONDON RECRUITS   LOCAL RECRUITS   RECRUITS FROM ELSEWHERE

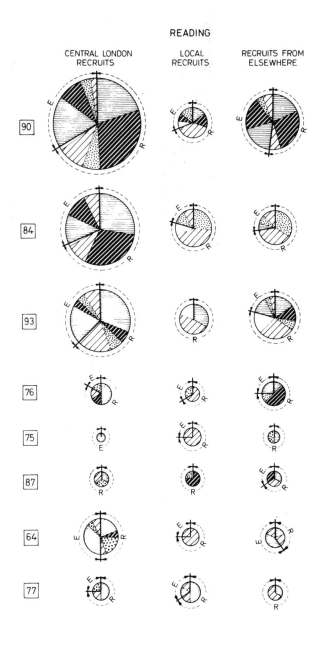

Figure 4.7   Initial residential location choice by relocating households, Reading offices

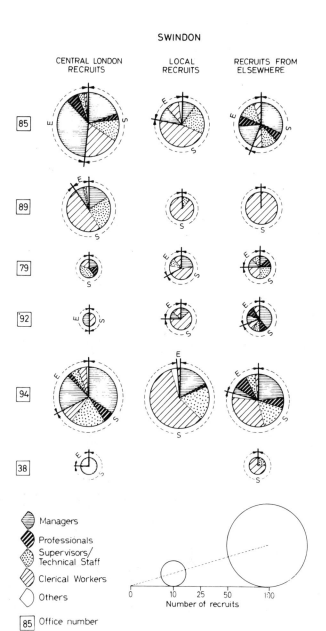

SWINDON

CENTRAL LONDON
RECRUITS

LOCAL
RECRUITS

RECRUITS FROM
ELSEWHERE

Managers
Professionals
Supervisors/
Technical Staff
Clerical Workers
Others

Number of recruits

85 Office number

S = Swindon   L = Liverpool   R = Reading   Sh = Southampton
W = Watford   E = Elsewhere

Figure 4.8   Initial residential location choice by
relocating households, Swindon offices

69

SOUTHAMPTON

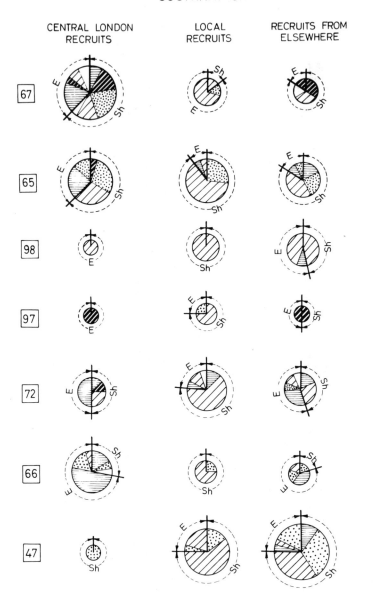

Figure 4.9   Initial residential location choice by relocating households, Southampton offices

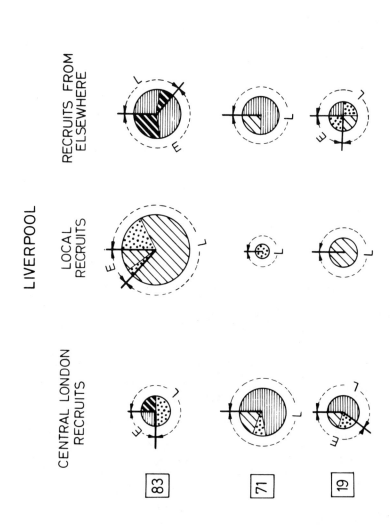

Figure 4.10 Initial residential location choice by relocating households, Liverpool offices

CHOICE OF DESTINATIONS BY MIGRANT HOUSEHOLDS

Information about the demand for housing in the reception centres is therefore confined to a consideration of the initial destinations chosen by the migrants shown in Figs. 4.1 - 4.5. The data has been illustrated for each office in each survey town and has been used to show that proportion of demand which is focused on the urban area to which the offices have relocated and that proportion which affects areas outside ('elsewhere' in the diagrams) (Figs. 4.6 - 4.10).[8] The administrative boundaries of each local authority have been used to distinguish between the urban area and elsewhere. This is an arbitrary distinction which works quite well for free-standing centres such as Swindon or Reading but is less satisfactory for Watford or Liverpool where there are large areas of contiguous urban development. An alternative procedure would be to devise a number of concentric zones around each centre but shortage of time has precluded the use of this procedure. The data illustrated in Figs. 4.6 - 4.10 relates to the residential location first chosen when migrants moved from the locations mapped in Figs. 4.1 - 4.5. Some employees have subsequently moved house again and, apart from those who occupy 'temporary' accommodation, this now represents housing demand which can be considered as internal to the local market. Clearly the principal concern here is with the character of externally derived demand for accommodation and it is therefore most useful to concentrate on primary residential location choice. A further question which arises in relation to the destinations chosen is whether occupation status and previous workplace of migrants affect the likelihood of searching and obtaining accommodation outside the reception centre? Therefore, the diagrams can be used to provide some guidance on this question. It was apparent in the Follow-Up Survey that residential change, which is to some degree connected with employment change, is not the prerogative of non-local recruits and therefore the residential choices or local recruits are also illustrated in Figs. 4.6 - 4.10.

The majority of the offices in Watford employ less than 50 people and this, combined with the proximity to central London, has clearly failed to generate a large number of migrants seeking housing in the area (Fig. 4.6). The Location of Offices Bureau study which included Watford also noted a low level of demand for housing by staff transferred to work in the area.[9] Most of the demand seems to have arisen from the relocation of the offices of a training board (office 96) and a food manufacturer (office 80). The pattern of demand by employees who have changed address is primarily oriented towards residential areas outside

Watford, particularly N.W. London. This applies in particular to managerial staff from areas outside Watford with over 75 percent of the movers in this group choosing non-Watford destinations. Clerical workers previously employed in central London also conform to this pattern but the sample is very limited and clerical workers from local sources and from elsewhere are more likely to be typical of the general tendency for these employees to favour residential areas within Watford. The majority of the moves by local recruits have been over short distances with origins and destinations within Watford; out-movement from Watford is the exception rather than the rule. Short distance office relocation to a centre such as Watford therefore generates low levels of housing demand and that which is created can be readily divided into those households which seek lower cost, smaller accommodation and who are most likely to choose residences in Watford, and those households which seek the higher cost, more exclusive properties. These are most sought by managers and professionals able to commute into Watford from outlying areas.

The demand for housing consequent upon relocation of offices to Reading is much more strongly focused on the reception areas than is the case at Watford (Fig. 4.7). The larger offices in the sample have again generated the greatest absolute demand, principally from central London recruits and employees from elsewhere. Taking all three groups of movers together, 68 percent have moved to or within Reading and this proportion applies equally to both groups of non-local recruits. The most likely to choose destinations in Reading are again clerical workers (74 percent) followed by employees in professional occupations (73 percent). Least likely to move into Reading are managers (60 percent) but because professionals and managers comprise such a large absolute share of the migrants they account for almost 60 percent of the total demand for houses in Reading by central London recruits and 53 percent by recruits from elsewhere. The data for the choices by office staff in the largest offices (90, 84 and 93) suggests that the occupation status of relocating employees does not necessarily polarize demand and managers and professionals are just as likely to move into Reading as they are into adjacent centres such as Henley-on-Thames, Pangbourne, Theale, Wokingham or Twyford. To some extent this also applies to the smaller offices. Almost all the demand for housing by local recruits is directed at properties within Reading where the majority are already resident but they only represent 16 percent of the total movers into Reading destinations.

The pressure of demand on Swindon rather than its surrounding area is even greater than at Reading (Fig. 4.8). Over 76 percent of all the movers have chosen residences within Swindon. Central London recruits (67 percent) are marginally less likely to move to Swindon, however, while recruits from elsewhere conform with the average distribution. On the other hand the anticipated dichotomy in residential location choice according to occupation status is more clearly expressed in Swindon than at Reading; 90 percent of the clerical workers and 82 percent of the supervisory/technical workers have moved to addresses located within Swindon compared with 61 and 53 percent respectively of the managerial and professional workers. The latter, as in Reading, comprise a significant proportion of the local sample of movers. Further, only some 30 percent of the demand for housing within Swindon emanates from these two groups compared with 66 percent outside Swindon.

A number of reasons can be advanced for the highly concentrated demand at Swindon. Firstly, it is a free-standing centre with only minor settlements some way down the urban hierarchy but within easy travelling distance (there is a wider range of alternative residential areas within daily travelling distance of Reading) and this reduces the effective residential search area for most office staff. Secondly, it may well be the case that because Swindon is an expanding town it does not have the diversity of housing accommodation which would satisfy the different demands of managerial compared with most clerical households in the way possible at Reading which has a more cosmopolitan housing stock. Thirdly, the larger employers mentioned that one consequence of Swindon's relatively isolated position is that it is not well serviced by public transport from outlying locations and, while this may not be an important negative factor for car-owning migrant households, this could have discouraged other households which would otherwise have done so from choosing residential accommodation outside the town. These are a few of the possible explanations but more satisfactory answers would undoubtedly have been obtained if it had been possible to pursue the extended interviews which had been originally planned. The limited material available here indicates that the type of urban area chosen by decentralized offices will, in addition to the occupation variable, influence the spatial pattern of housing demand.

Following the above reasoning, it would be expected that the results for Southampton migrants would be most likely to resemble the structure of demand at Reading and this is indeed the case (Fig. 4.9). The principal occupational difference between Reading and Southampton is the lower proportion of managers and professionals so that they comprise a much lower share of overall demand both within Southampton (15 percent) and outside (45 percent). That demand which does exist is concentrated on locations outside Southampton, particularly by office employees in managerial positions; only 30 percent reside in Southampton but the figure for professionals is similar to that for Reading at 62 percent. Rather more of the central London recruits have also opted for locations outside Southampton than would be expected from the Reading results. Hence, marginally fewer households overall (64 percent) have moved into or within Southampton. Most of the 'internal' demand emanates from local recruits; almost exclusively clerical workers. Almost all the central London recruits in managerial occupations have chosen residential areas outside Southampton and over 50 percent of the recruits from elsewhere. As expected, the majority (60-70 percent) of clerical staff from both sources have moved to Southampton itself.

The sample of movers at Liverpool is very limited but the information which is available shows that most of the demand is focused on Liverpool and the areas classified as 'elsewhere' are almost exclusively within the contiguous built-up area of Merseyside County (Fig. 4.10). It is the size and diversity of the city rather than its isolation which accounts for the fact that 79 percent of the movers have chosen locations within Liverpool. There are only minor differences between occupation groups although almost 70 percent of the clerical workers, most of whom are local recruits, have remained in the same area. The data available for three of the case study offices shows that central London recruits have primarily moved to Liverpool irrespective of status and the pattern is similar for recruits from other parts of the country, except for the largest office (83) in which managers and professionals have a clear bias towards residential areas outside the District.

It has been shown that the critical determinants of the volume of demand for housing at reception centres are office staff brought in from elsewhere and from central London. The aggregate data for all five towns shows that for every one employee in this category who initially chose to live outside each centre, two will seek housing accommodation within the principal urban area. Occupation status does influence the spatial character of demand but the particular characteristics of each reception centre, such as its location and diversity of housing stock, can modify the important effect of occupation status on residential choice. It seems that proximity to London enhances the contrasts

in residential choice by different occupation groups
but further from London an increase in the diversity
of housing stock improves the scope for demand by
all occupation groups which is centred primarily on
the urban area into which the offices have moved.
It must be stressed again, however, that these are
inferred rather than precisely measured conclusions
because it has not been possible to examine the decision
making process of the individual households which
have created the residential distribution observed
at each of the study centres.

TEMPORAL ASPECTS OF HOUSING DEMAND

There is also a time dimension to the demand for housing
in the reception towns and this has two principal
causes. Firstly, offices usually move to an area
over a period of several years so that the expressed
demand in any one year will depend on the size and
occupation structure of in-migrant organisations as
well as of those offices already well established.
Secondly, the demand for housing does not begin and
end just before and after an office moves but can
be spread over several years. All the employees who
make residential changes do not do so for reasons
connected with the location of their place of employment
while recruitment by the decentralized establishment
to add to or to replace its staff complement will
also continue. In order to see whether the long term
trends in the demand for housing contain some significant
features the data discussed in the preceding section
of this chapter been reorganised in such a way that
the initial move of each employee is expressed in
years before or after the relocation of their existing
place of employment. The data has been further stratified
according to previous workplace in order to test the
assumption that the major share of demand generated
by central London recruits and office workers from
other parts of the country occur immediately before
and shortly after decentralization has taken place.

Annual demands for housing by workers in decentralized
offices reveal a distinctive bi-modal distribution
(Fig. 4.11). Although as anticipated, the largest
share of total demand is concentrated in the years
immediately before and after the offices have moved,
there is also a substantial secondary peak which occurs
some 7-10 years after the office relocations are completed. Hence, 43 percent of all relocating households
in the five towns completed their initial moves within
12 months either side of office relocation but a further
24 percent were completed much later. It should be
noted, however, that if moves completed within 2 years
following decentralization are included then over 55

76

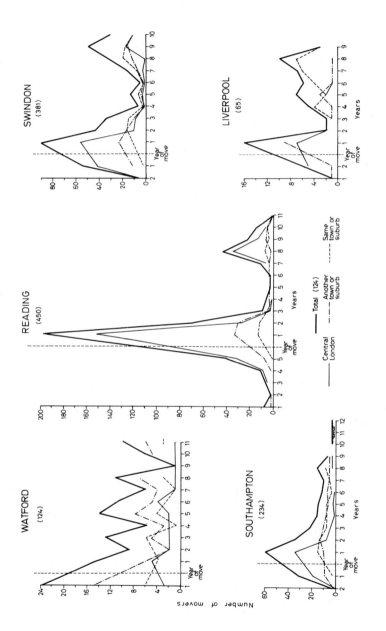

Figure 4.11 Annual demand for housing by office workers in the five study towns

percent of the demand can be directly attributed to the office relocation decision. There are differences between the centres with respect to the clarity of the bi-modal distribution. In Reading 53 percent of the demand is in the first group and 21 percent in the latter; for Swindon the equivalent figures are 38 percent and 34 percent and for Southampton 39 and 15 percent.

These variations are linked to the origins of the demand for housing. Reading and Swindon both have large numbers of central London recruits and 62 percent and 60 percent of them, respectively, moved to these areas within 12 months either side of office relocation. This is similar to the average for all five towns which is 62 percent for central London recruits. Only 18 percent moved during the later period. Recruits from elsewhere show a more even pattern of demand with 33 percent overall in the first period and 24 percent in the. latter. The variations in the curves for this group will depend on whether they were previously employed by the same organisation and the importance of the decentralized establishment for their employment. Some organisations deploy staff from other locations at the same time as decentralization is being undertaken while others, including the Civil Service, may do so over extended periods of time as part of a policy of moving employees around for promotional purposes or for providing experience in different departments. It is not unexpected that local recruits are least likely to undertake residential changes at the same time as they join the labour force of decentralized offices; 18 percent are in the first group and 36 percent in the latter. These average figures disguise the considerable variation in this basic distribution; in Watford almost a third of local recruits moved during the first period and 24 percent at Southampton while the pattern at the other three centres is more similar to the overall distribution for local recruits.

The results for each centre will not be discussed separately because the principal differences between them are linked to the magnitude of demand rather than the pattern through time. As offices expand, undertake phased relocations, or staff turnover generates the need for replacements they create demand for housing over several years far removed from the initial relocation decision. If this recruitment activity involves bringing in staff from outside the local area, as it certainly appears to on the basis of the evidence obtained in this survey, then office decentralization does not create a "once and for all" demand for housing; rather is may consist of a number of peaks and troughs according to the recruitment cycles of companies or, for local recruits, according to life-cycle circumstances.

Table 4.2

Relationship between residential mobility and travel mode choice, trip time, trip distance and present occupation — offices in survey towns

Travel mode, trip time, trip distance	Survey towns				
	Watford	Reading	Swindon	Southampton	Liverpool
TRAVEL MODE					
X^2	5.28*[1]	32.20	46.81	16.31	15.82
C^2	0.10	0.15	0.20	0.16	0.22
TRIP TIME					
X^2	3.75*	51.69	1.53*	5.85*	5.18*
C	0.09	0.19	0.04	0.09	0.13
TRIP DISTANCE					
X^2	28.87	23.66	32.09	10.74	15.32
C	0.24	0.13	0.17	0.13	0.22
OCCUPATION STATUS					
X^2	28.20	62.59	37.22	27.64	21.65
C	0.24	0.21	0.18	0.21	0.26

Notes: 1. Values of X^2 which are not significant at the 0.5 percent level.
         H_o = No difference in travel mode choice, trip time, trip distance or occupation status with respect to whether an employee has changed address since taking up employment at the decentralized office.

         2. Contingency coefficient.

Source: Office Survey, 1976.

In the context of the journey to work it is possible that office workers who make residential changes are in some way distinctive from those who do not (Table 4.2). The values of X^2 for occupation status in relation to whether respondents are movers or non-movers all permit the null hypothesis (specified in Table 4.2) to be rejected and, along with the associated values of C, permit the conclusion that higher status office staff are more likely to change residence than other groups. This being the case there should be a significant relationship between travel mode and movers/non-movers with the former, in view of their occupation status, more likely to be car owners. It is only possible to accept the null hypothesis for the Watford respondents. The C values are low, however, and suggest a weak association between the two variables which is also demonstrated for journey to work times. Watford is the only centre with a significant difference between movers and non-movers in terms of trip times for the journey to work. The distinction between movers and non-movers is best measured with reference to distance travelled to work; all values of X^2 are significant at the 0.5 percent level and C is reasonably high for Watford, Swindon and Liverpool. Since managers and professionals are prominent amongst the movers this result is consistent with the probability that more of this group will reside further from their work places than other groups of staff.

CONCLUSION

This chapter has probably raised more questions than it has answered. Some of the questions have already been posed earlier and a number of others also appear important. The material discussed here has concentrated on initial moves by householders but it was shown in the Follow-Up Survey that almost 40 percent of the mover households made two or more residential changes during the period after office relocation was completed.[10] Therefore, this prompts questions about both the motivations for these changes and their spatial consequences. Are they primarily short distance "adjustments" subsequent to the accumulation of better knowledge about housing opportunities in the reception towns or is there a tendency to move initially into the town concerned and then to move out again to the surrounding area, so promoting urban decentralization and an extension of labour catchment areas? Does the residential relocation behaviour of local recruits differ from that of in-migrants and is it generally unconnected to the decision to accept employment in a newly decentralized office? Which sections of the housing market have to face the main effects of the demand from migrant office workers and do the changes which they make create improved living conditions and lower costs? What part does the journey to work play in post-decentralization residential changes? Other items could be added to this list and it would have been possible to answer some of them if it had been feasible to follow through the programme of work which had been planned. There is scope for further research on this subject and perhaps it may be possible to undertake further work in the future.

NOTES AND REFERENCES

(1) E. Hammond, London to Durham : A Study of the Transfer Of the Post Office Savings Certificate Division, Rowntree Research Unit, Durham 1968; S.J. Carey, Relocation of Office Staff : A Study of the Reactions of Staff Decentralized to Ashford, Location of Offices Bureau, Research Paper No. 4, London 1969; D. Burtenshaw and R.K. Hall, Office Staff on the Move, Location of Offices Bureau, Research Paper No. 6, London 1971; M. Bateman, D. Burtenshaw and A. Duffett, 'Rehousing migrant office workers', Paper presented at Frist Anglo-German Geographical Seminar, Giessen, Wunsberg, München, April 1973; E. Sidwell, 'London to Bristol' : the experience of a major office organisation and its staff', in P.W. Daniels (ed.), Spatial Patterns of Office Growth and Location, Wiley, London 1979, pp. 349-72.

(2) M. Bateman and D. Burtenshaw 'The social effects of office decentralization', in P.W. Daniels (ed.), op. cit., pp. 325-48.

(3) E. Hammond, op. cit.; M. Bateman and D. Burtenshaw, The Impact of Office Decentralization to a Provincial Centre, Social Science Research Council (Final Report), London 1975.

(4) For a useful overview and bibliography see J.M. Quigley and D.H. Weinberg, 'Intra-urban residential mobility : a review and synthesis', International Regional Science Review, Vol. 2, 1977 pp. 41-66.

(5) M. Bateman, D. Burtenshaw and A. Duffett, 'Environmental perception and migration : a study of perception of residential areas in South Hampshire' in D. Carter and T. Lee (eds.), Psychology and the Built Environment, Architectural Press, London 1974.

(6) M. Bateman and D. Burtenshaw, op. cit., 1979.

(7) Over 50 percent of the respondents to the Follow-
     Up and Office Centre Survey indicated that
     they would be prepared to participate in a
     further interview if required at a later date.

(8) The Key for Figs. 4.6 - 4.10 is included with
     Fig. 4.8 (Swindon).

(9) Location of Offices Bureau, Demand and Supply
     for Office Workers and the Local Impact of
     Office Development, Report prepared by Economic
     Consultants Ltd., Location of Offices Bureau,
     London 1971, p. 79.

5 Spatial and temporal attributes of the journey to work of office staff

The next two chapters are devoted to a discussion of the journey to work patterns generated by the offices in each study centre. All journey to work distances are expressed as airline distance between origin and destination and for some office workers in Liverpool and Southampton this produces some under-estimation of true trip distance because of the barrier effect of the estuaries, especially in Southampton.[1] The number of employees affected in this way is limited however, and it has not been considered worthwhile to calculate a sample of actual route distances in order to correct these errors. Trip times are derived from the aggregate of the times indicated by respondents for each stage of their work journeys (see Appendix). It is therefore likely that for some respondents this also creates an underestimate of their total trip time because all respondents have clearly not recorded all the stages in their journeys. Therefore, if a waiting stage between bus connections has not been recorded on the questionnaire, for example, several minutes are probably overlooked. Some indication of the scale of under-reporting of trip stages, and therefore trip time, is provided by the large number of office workers who claim to have single stage work trips; even car drivers must walk from their parking places to their offices; few parking places are so proximal to office buildings that a short walk is not required.[2] Assuming that these deficiencies are distributed in a similar way throughout the survey population, it is probably reasonable to conclude that their effect on the trip time curves discussed below will be to reduce the amplitude rather than to cause a major change in the shape of the curves. If this is accepted then the data can be taken as a reasonable approximation of the 'true' trip time distributions.

JOURNEY TO WORK TIMES AND DISTANCES

The well established dichotomy between the journey to work distances of male and female office workers is well illustrated in all five centres (Fig. 5.1).[3] The differences between the values of C for Watford (0.27) or Reading (0.25) and for Southampton (0.31) and Liverpool (0.34) indicate that the association

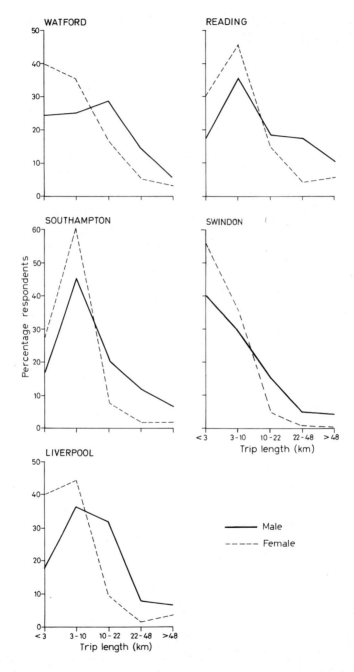

Figure 5.1   Journey to work distances for male and female
office workers in the study towns

between sex and trip distance is likely to be better in provincial centres; a circumstance which is reinforced by the probability that decentralized offices in these areas will employ more female supervisory and clerical workers than offices in centres nearer to London.[4] The majority of journeys to work by female office staff are under 22km in length and in all the centres, except Watford, the largest proportion of journeys originate from within 3-10km of the offices. Comparison of the curves in Fig. 5.1 with those for the four case study offices in the Follow-Up Survey suggests that the trip distance distributions for the journey to work of both male and female office workers in decentralized offices can now be predicted with some confidence.[5] The curves for one office in New Malden (S.W. London) and one in Southampton are similar to those in Fig. 5.1.

With the exception of Swindon, between 25 and 40 percent of female office workers travel less than 3km while only 20 percent of male office workers reside so close to their offices. In Swindon over 56 percent of the female staff travel less than 3km and almost twice as many males (40 percent) as in the other survey towns. Although a further 35-45 percent of male employees also reside within 3-10km of their offices the tail of the trip distance curves is both less steep and represents a larger proportion of total journeys than for females. The clearest difference between male and female distributions occurs at Watford where the majority of male trips (29 percent) are grouped in the 10-22km band compared with 40 percent of females with trip origins inside the 3km band. A difference of similar order also occurs in Liverpool.

By combining the curves for males and females and comparing them with the aggregated curves for all five centres it emerges that Watford and Swindon have considerably more journeys of less than 3km, 32 percent of all trips in the five centres, than expected (156/152 and 535/343). The discrepancy is particularly large in Swindon which seems to have the most compact office labour catchment areas of any of the centres. Intermediate origins between 3-22km are over-represented in Reading, as expected, and also in Liverpool mainly because of the residential distribution of male office workers. Another compact journey to work area occurs in Southampton where there are fewer trips than expected from within 3km of the offices but considerably more in the 3-10km range (326/239). Long distance journeys to work (over 22km) create the most dispersed labour catchments in Reading and Watford, especially the former with trips of more than 22km occurring in the ratio 289/186. These trips occur with less frequency than expected from the overall distribution for the

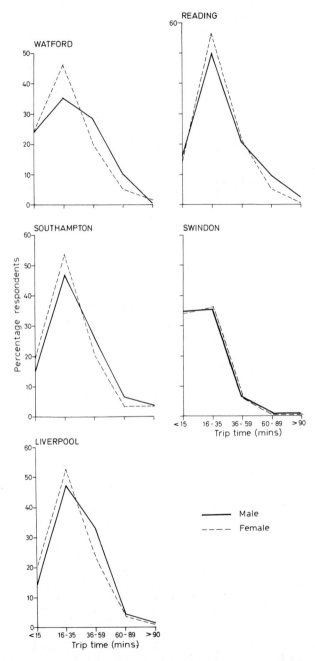

Figure 5.2   Trip times for the journeys to work of male
             and female office workers in the study towns.

sample at both Southampton and Liverpool and, most categorically, in Swindon where there are only half as many trips of more than 22km as expected.

The results of a similar exercise in the Follow-Up Study leads to the expectation that the distinctive spatial distribution of male and female trip origins will not be paralleled by the distribution of trip times for the journey to work.[6] This assumption is clearly corroborated by the data in Fig. 5.2 and given further support by the much lower values of C, which range between 0.12 and 0.16, and do not display the trend towards a strengthening of relationship between sex and trip time in urban areas furthest from London evident for trip distances. As expected from the value of C (0.16) the discrepancy between the trip times of males and females is largest in Watford mainly because long trips of more than one hour account for more than 12 percent of the male journeys to work. The journey times of employees in the Follow-up Survey are more positively skewed towards trips lasting less than 15 minutes (31 percent compared with 25 percent in the study towns).[7] This probably arises from the way in which it emerged in the Follow-Up Survey that office employee catchment areas have tended to become more compact in 1976 when compared with 1969 and this characteristic has not yet had a chance to develop fully for those offices in the present study which relocated between 1973 and 1975. The differences would have been larger if Swindon, which has an unusually large proportion of short trips, had not been included in the survey.

The differences between observed and expected trip time curves for all employees in each centre are therefore much smaller than those for trip distances, most of them amount to between 15-20 trips, a difference which could reasonably be attributed to chance variations amongst the respondents. Swindon is again the principal exception with far more journeys to work than expected taking less than 15 minutes (469/269) and large discrepancies in the number of more time consuming trips. Trips of less than 15 minutes duration are marginally under-represented in Watford and Liverpool but at Reading the difference is much larger than average (220/344). In Watford there are fewer trips than expected in the 16-35 minutes category and this no doubt reflects the more difficult commuting conditions in this area which is well inside commuting distances to London. On the basis of the distribution of trip origins it is not surprising that journeys to work lasting more than 60 minutes occur with a higher observed frequency in Watford, Reading and, marginally, Southampton with Reading having the largest surplus (144/102).

OCCUPATION STATUS, PREVIOUS WORKPLACE AND TRIP TIMES/
DISTANCES

The basic distinction between male and female journey
to work characteristics does not take adequate account,
as we have seen in earlier chapters, of the variations
in trip characteristics which are attributable to
occupation status and to the place of recruitment
of office staff. An attempt has been made to examine
some of these variations in a series of tabulations
(Tables 5.1 - 5.4) in which male and female journeys
to work are disaggregated by mean time and mean distance
according to previous workplace classification and
occupation status. A comparison of the mean values
shown in the tables may be misleading, however, unless
they are related in some way to the distribution of
the observations which have contributed to them.
The standard deviation (S) is the usual measure but
this alone does not permit an examination of the difference or similarity between the various sub-groups
of the total population. Therefore the coefficient
of variability (V) has been used to provide a more
objective indication of the homogeneity of the sub-
groups which have different means and standard devia-
tions.[8] In the present context it would also be useful
if the number of observations in each sub-group could
be incorporated in the calculation of V; some groups
include less than 10 respondents. The confidence
which can be placed in V probably increases with the
size of sample as it does for S and $\bar{X}$.

The results for mean trip distances by previous
workplace (Table 5.1) and occupation status (Table
5.2) show firstly, that for both males and females
there is extensive variation around the mean values
and, secondly, that there is considerably homogeneity
within the broad sub-groups of males and females.
This is the case even though it is clear that the
mean distances travelled are often very different.
Hence, male local recruits in all five centres travel
only half as far to work on average as recruits brought
in from other parts of the country but there is still
considerable similarity between them in terms of the
range of origins which are summarised by the mean
value. A similar phenomenon is illustrated by female
central London staff when compared with female local
recruits. There is also considerable homogeneity
in the distribution of trip distances according to
occupation status, with the exception of clerical
workers. Both male and female clerical workers in
almost every centre have consistently higher values
of V than the norm for the male/female sub-group.
This suggests that, contrary to expectations, some
clerical workers are often prepared to travel longer
distances to obtain employment than the average journey

88

Table 5.1

Mean trip distances by sex and previous workplace

Sex and Previous Workplace		Watford		Reading		Survey Towns Swindon		Southampton		Liverpool	
		$\bar{d}$	V^1	$\bar{d}$	V	$\bar{d}$	V	$\bar{d}$	V	$\bar{d}$	V
MALES		(206)²		(807)		(424)		(275)		(108)	
Central London	PE³	14.1 *	1.012	17.7	1.032	10.8	1.475	21.1	1.165	20.8	1.210
	AE⁴	14.2 *	1.284	16.3	1.044	14.6	1.632	17.7 *	0.968	8.9 *	1.037
Local recruits	PE	13.1	1.301	5.2 *	0.933	9.9	2.176	6.8	0.851	7.2	0.884
	AE	11.3	2.185	11.5	1.576	5.4	1.577	5.8	0.858	8.6	0.579
Elsewhere	PE	19.4	1.179	24.1	1.009	15.2	1.746	17.3	1.191	13.1 *	0.771
	AE	18.6	1.127	19.5	1.064	16.1	1.239	12.7	1.212	13.8	1.235
NPE⁵		11.6	0.800	9.1	1.480	6.2	1.747	11.3	1.891	10.1	0.868
FEMALES		(248)		(501)		(628)		(297)		(176)	
Central London	PE	14.9	1.329	10.6	1.354	7.1	1.579	7.4	0.735	--	--
	AE	8.5	1.264	7.1	1.318	5.6	0.791	46.1	1.176	--	--
Local recruits	PE	4.7	1.100	3.9	0.893	3.2	0.743	4.6	0.804	6.0	0.651
	AE	7.7	2.056	5.8	1.240	4.2	1.544	4.6	0.712	6.1	1.596
Elsewhere	PE	8.9	0.629	16.9 *	1.097	4.8	0.908	10.4	0.975	14.6 *	0.927
	AE	6.9	0.965	10.1	0.999	9.6	1.534	7.3	0.665	11.2 *	0.929
NPE		7.1	1.498	8.1	1.313	3.8	2.318	4.9	0.617	6.9	2.070
Total Population		11.1	1.459	13.3	1.252	6.8	1.880	9.6	1.513	8.7	1.456

Notes: 1. Coefficient of variability (s.d./$\bar{d}$).
         2. Number of observations.
         3. Present employer.
         4. Some other employer.
         5. Not previously employed.
         *   Denotes < 10 observations.

Source: Office Survey, 1976.

89

Table 5.2

Mean trip distances by sex and occupation status

Survey Towns

Sex and Occupation Status	Watford		Reading		Swindon		Southampton		Liverpool	
	$\bar{d}$	V¹	$\bar{d}$	V	$\bar{d}$	V	$\bar{d}$	V	$\bar{d}$	V
MALES	15.1	1.263 (213)²	16.5	1.134 (816)	10.2	1.677 (421)	13.1	1.348 (295)	11.8	1.168 (112)
Managerial	18.8	1.105	19.2	1.005	14.5	1.475	20.8	1.196	16.6	1.157
Professional	15.5	1.132	16.2	1.170	11.0	1.443	10.0	0.775	8.1 * 0.881	
Supervisory etc.	13.3	1.190	13.5	1.176	7.6	1.400	9.5	1.150	9.9	0.699
Clerical	9.2	1.701	14.5	1.330	6.6	2.205	10.8	1.420	8.0	0.759
Other	8.8	2.422	7.0	1.663	3.5	0.846	8.8 * 0.731		1.4 * 0.721	
FEMALES	7.6	1.554 (256)	8.0	1.311 (503)	4.5	1.805 (637)	5.7	1.196 (300)	6.8	1.680 (177)
Managerial	15.6	0.804	16.1	1.216	6.7	1.254	5.1 * 0.427		11.1 * 0.768	
Professional	2.2 * –		6.5	1.034	1.7 *0.239		–	–	–	–
Supervisory etc.	10.9	1.986	8.8	1.100	6.2	1.383	6.5	0.986	9.4	1.801
Clerical	6.3	1.547	7.6	1.290	4.3	1.922	5.7	1.234	6.4	1.633
Other	3.0	0.423	3.8	0.521	1.3	0.801	3.5 * 0.466		2.7 * 0.584	
Total population	11.0	1.452	13.2	1.250	6.8	1.888	9.4	1.476	8.7	1.443

Notes:
1. Coefficient of variability (s.d./$\bar{d}$).
2. Number of observations.
* Denotes < 10 observations.

Source: Office Survey, 1976.

Table 5.3

Mean trip times by sex and previous workplace

Sex and Previous Workplace		Survey Towns									
		Watford		Reading		Swindon		Southampton		Liverpool	
		t̄	v[1]	t̄	v	t̄	v	t̄	v	t̄	v
MALES		32.9 (206)	0.616	35.0 (824)	0.754	21.3 (430)	0.899	36.3 (279)	0.944	31.8 (113)	0.560
Central London	PE[3]	33.4	0.662	37.0	0.806	22.8	0.948	43.4	1.264	47.9	0.576
	AE[4]	34.2	0.658	32.1	0.642	19.7	0.710	41.7 *	0.389	22.2 *	0.697
Local recruits	PE	27.7	0.632	29.2 *	0.485	24.0	1.193	29.7	0.633	26.2	0.523
	AE	26.2	0.682	27.6	0.553	17.7	0.590	30.8	0.664	30.7	0.389
Elsewhere	PE	34.1	0.594	39.3	0.729	18.7	0.687	38.9	0.490	42.1 *	0.267
	AE	35.4	0.582	35.0	0.666	23.9	0.567	33.1	0.611	26.1	0.504
NPE[5]		32.9	0.565	31.3	0.671	20.9	1.162	33.0	0.705	27.7	0.536
FEMALES		30.1 (251)	0.648	30.8 (519)	0.583	21.1 (625)	0.690	30.3 (301)	0.653	29.5 (178)	0.521
Central London	PE	35.3 *	0.371	30.3	0.534	24.8	0.924	29.8	0.614	–	–
	AE	40.0 *	0.926	23.2	0.520	19.5	0.540	49.0 *	0.173	–	–
Local recruits	PE	31.9	0.608	26.3	0.453	22.7	0.671	28.8	0.852	27.3	0.446
	AE	28.0	0.651	28.3	0.497	20.4	0.745	30.0	0.607	28.9	0.513
Elsewhere	PE	34.0	0.488	42.7 *	0.626	24.6	0.781	31.3	0.704	44.7 *	0.391
	AE	27.4	0.530	33.5	0.566	23.1	0.560	32.4	0.683	32.5 *	0.579
NPE		32.1	0.730	33.2	0.628	19.4	0.625	30.1	0.659	29.7	0.547
Total population		31.4	0.634	33.4	0.706	21.2	0.782	33.2	0.839	30.4	0.539

Notes:
1. Coefficient of variability (s.d./d̄).
2. Number of observations.
3. Present employer.
4. Some other employer.
5. Not previously employed.
* Denotes < 10 observations

Source: Office Survey, 1976.

Table 5.4

Mean trip times by sex and occupation status

Sex and Occupation Status	Survey Towns									
	Watford		Reading		Swindon		Southampton		Liverpool	
	$\bar{t}$	V^1	$\bar{t}$	V	$\bar{t}$	V	$\bar{t}$	V	$\bar{t}$	V
MALES	(214)²		(836)		(426)		(299)		(294)	
33.6 / 0.723	33.6	0.723	34.9	0.753	21.2	0.903	36.1	0.930	32.4	0.553
Managerial	36.7	0.748	37.9	0.836	23.3	0.980	41.9	1.299	37.9	0.522
Professional	32.1	0.500	33.4	0.721	19.7	0.586	31.4	0.663	15.6 *	0.576
Supervisory etc.	34.7	0.656	31.9	0.580	19.0	0.596	34.8	0.633	31.3	0.494
Clerical	30.7	0.734	34.1	0.626	21.9	1.011	34.0	0.590	30.0	0.406
Other	19.0	0.504	27.4	0.630	15.6	0.641	32.5 *	0.518	15.5 *	1.062
FEMALES	(258)		(632)		(303)		(178)			
30.4 / 0.643	30.4	0.643	30.8	0.583	21.0	0.690	30.7	0.670	29.6	0.517
Managerial	39.7	0.548	34.9	0.621	25.1	0.995	25.0 *	0.400	28.3 *	0.620
Professional	14.0 *	–	23.8	0.619	14.0 *	0.767	–	–	–	–
Supervisory etc.	31.3	0.686	30.9	0.521	19.2	0.529	26.5	0.592	27.4	0.564
Clerical	28.8	0.638	30.9	0.593	21.2	0.679	31.2	0.681	30.1	0.510
Other	33.7	0.729	26.7	0.436	20.4	0.885	32.9 *	0.540	26.3 *	0.562
Total population	31.8	0.686	33.3	0.706	21.1	0.783	33.4	0.837	30.7	0.534

Number of observations (in parentheses) for MALES: Watford (214)², Reading (836), Swindon (426), Southampton (299), Liverpool (294); for FEMALES: Watford (258), Reading (518), Swindon (632), Southampton (303), Liverpool (178).

Notes:
1. Coefficient of variability (s.d./$\bar{t}$).
2. Number of observations.
* Denotes < 10 observations.

Source: Office Survey, 1976.

92

to work distances for the group (which are almost always half those of managerial staff) suggest. It may be, of course, that clerical occupations contain a wider spectrum of age, ability and income than some other occupation groups and this means that the more senior, and often older, office staff can live in areas further removed from their offices than expected. It is suggested, however, that such a situation is atypical and does not greatly distort the differences in residential distribution implied by the statistics in Table 5.1.

A number of other observations can be gleaned from Tables 5.1 and 5.2. Firstly, the values of V for each study centre suggest rather less homogeneity between them than that which is found within them. Hence, the values for male office staff in Swindon (1.67) and for females (1.80) are much higher than for Reading (1.13 and 1.31 respectively). This may indicate that the more centralized pattern of office location in the Reading sample is conducive to a more constrained journey to work pattern than at Swindon where the wide spread of locations encourages greater variation in workplace/residence relationships even though it is quite possible that the average distance of households from the centre of Swindon is no higher than at Reading. Secondly, female office workers display more variation between, as well as within, centres than male office workers with a range from 1.80 in Swindon to 1.19 in Southampton and from 1.17 to 1.69 in Liverpool. The latter is the widest difference but some of the other centres, such as Watford, also have a large discrepancy. The fact that some female office staff are dependent on others such as their husbands or friends/colleagues for access to employment opportunities and particularly for transport to that employment again seems to have the effect of introducing more variability than basic averages would lead us to expect and this factor may also help to explain why some of the V values for female local recruits and clerical workers are near or above 2.0 in some cases. If females were dependent on their own salaries they would not be able to commute such long distances but husbands in jobs which permit them to make longer journeys to work provide the transport opportunities. Females can travel to work as car passengers or partici-pate in car sharing in a way which tends to extend the dispersal of trip origins around the mean.

A third observation arising from Table 5.1 is that, with few exceptions, office staff who previously worked for their present employer (PE) have longer journeys to work than recruits from other employers. This relates primarily to central London recruits and those

93

brought in from elsewhere. The implication here is
that although we can normally expect these two groups
to change address if decentralization merits it, it
is also likely that if at all possible, they will
not do so and this helps to generate longer work journeys
than recruits from other employers (AE) who are, amongst
other things, probably attracted by the possibility
of shorter journeys to work. The reverse seems to
be the case for local recruits, however, since some
employers will offer higher salaries in order to induce
new staff to join them from other employers tapping
the same labour market with the result that the catchment
area tends to be extended beyond that typical for
their own employees (PE) already resident in the survey
towns. Fourthly, it should be noted that employees
entering employment for the first time or returning
after a period away from work, in order to start a
family for example, often travel further than local
recruits as a whole. Perhaps this is symptomatic
of the shortage of jobs as a result of national economic
conditions during 1973-76 which has caused this group
to look further afield for work than expected. The
values of V are also near to or above the average
for males/females and tend to support this hypothesis.

A similar exercise using mean trip times reveals
less variability both between centres and within sub-
groups of office employees in each survey town (Tables
5.3 and 5.4). It is also apparent that there is a
much narrower difference between the mean and standard
deviation for trip times; there are only a few values
of V which exceed 1.0 and the majority are in the
range 0.45-0.65. Although the mean trip times of
female office workers are only just lower than for
male office workers in all five centres the values
of V show that there is less variation around the
mean time than is the case for males. As well as
having the lowest journey distances, Swindon respondents
also have the lowest mean journey times with values
almost identical for males and females (21 minutes).
The differences between sub-groups on the basis of
previous workplace are also less marked than at some
of the other centres. Central London recruits at
Watford have journey times some 6-7 minutes longer
on average than local recruits; a difference which
also occurs between the latter and recruits from elsewhere.
The effect of travel cost concessions on trip times
is evident at Southampton where the mean journey to
work times of central London recruits are 12-13 minutes
higher than those of local staff.

With reference to occupation status the values of
V for the male sub-groups indicate a lower level of
homogeneity than that displayed by the female office
workers (Table 5.4). Swindon and Southampton have

Table 5.5

Summary of trip time and trip distance distribution for the journey to work
by occupation and previous workplace of office staff in survey towns

Trip time (mins) and trip distance (km)		Occupation status[1]				Previous workplace			
		Managerial	Professional	Supervisory	Clerical	Central London	Local	Elsewhere	NPE[2]
WATFORD	t <35	50.4	57.9	63.4	73.6	61.5	74.4	58.7	63.3
	t >60	13.0	—	14.1	6.9	15.4	6.1	9.7	13.4
	d <10	35.9	47.4	60.6	79.7	47.7	79.9	52.3	68.3
	d >22	27.4	15.8	18.3	5.2	13.8	11.0	20.0	10.1
READING	t <35	60.7	69.6	72.5	70.9	66.0	78.9	59.7	68.7
	t >60	14.8	13.2	10.0	7.2	12.4	2.1	15.7	9.4
	d <10	47.7	56.6	62.0	71.3	54.1	85.1	47.0	71.6
	d >22	34.2	27.5	16.9	12.0	27.9	5.0	32.2	11.8
SWINDON	t <35	86.5	89.8	93.9	90.4	92.9	90.9	86.8	88.7
	t >60	4.1	4.0	1.1	2.0	3.6	2.1	3.0	1.4
	d <10	59.0	78.5	80.2	91.2	70.6	92.1	62.9	94.3
	d >22	18.2	10.2	7.6	2.7	12.7	1.9	19.8	2.5
SOUTHAMPTON	t <35	62.0	70.0	68.2	67.8	60.9	73.4	59.7	69.5
	t >60	10.3	6.6	10.3	9.2	12.2	4.7	11.6	7.8
	d <10	48.2	60.0	74.7	82.4	47.8	89.7	61.2	87.0
	d >22	29.8	16.7	10.3	6.4	27.0	1.3	19.4	6.0
LIVERPOOL	t <35	54.0	100.0	67.2	70.3	54.5	71.4	60.9	72.0
	t >60	8.0	—	6.9	3.5	18.2	2.0	4.9	4.9
	d <10	40.0	60.0	63.8	84.3	40.9	83.0	51.2	75.6
	d >22	18.0	—	13.8	4.7	18.2	3.4	24.4	8.6

Notes: 1. The small number of 'Other' employees are excluded.
        2. Not previously employed.

Source: Office Survey, 1976

95

the widest range of V values and therefore the least
homogeneous samples with a range for males from 1.29
for those in managerial occupations to 0.51 for the
'other' occupations at offices in the latter centre.
In general, however, clerical workers have the lowest
values of V and reveal least variation between centres
when compared with the equivalent statistics for managerial and professional workers.

The spatial distribution of office employees in
each centre according to their occupation status and
previous workplace is summarised in Table 5.5. With
the exception of Liverpool and Swindon (18 percent)
over 25 percent of the managers in the sample travel
more than 22km to work with Reading having the highest
value of 34 percent. Less than half the managers
in all the centres except Swindon travel less than
10km. Between 55 and 60 percent of the employees
in professional occupations (who are not well represented
in this survey) travel less than 10km rising to 60-
70 percent of the supervisory and related office staff.
Less than 1 in 5 of the latter are likely to travel
more than 22km but the ratio is even lower for clerical
workers at approximately 1 in 10 compared with 7 in
10 travelling to work from within 10km of their offices.
The highest values, more than 8 in 10, occur in Southampton and Liverpool.

In view of the relationship already shown between
occupation status and previous workplace the spatial
pattern of trip origins for the latter largely reflects
the residential distribution of office workers according
to their occupation status. It is not the central
London recruits, however, who generate the largest
proportion of trips exceeding 22km; it is recruits
from other parts of the country, especially those
employed in Reading and Swindon who generate a large
proportion of trips in this category (approximately
1 in 5 for all the centres). This is in marked contrast
to local recruits almost all of whom have journeys
to work which are less than 10km. Since most of the
respondents in this group already had journeys to
work of similar length prior to the establishment
of the decentralized offices, the scope for generating
wider journey to work benefits is likely to be in
inverse ratio to the number of local recruits employed
by relocating organisations. The larger the number
of central London and/or recruits from elsewhere,
the clearer the tangible improvements in the journey
to work.

The summary figures in Table 5.5 also show that
supervisory and clerical office workers are only half
as likely to spend more than one hour on the journey
to work as managerial or professional staff in Watford,

Table 5.6

Trip distance and trip times for full-time and part-time office staff – Watford and Liverpool

Trip distance (km) and trip time (mins)	Survey town[3]				Overall trip distance distribution (all towns)
	Watford		Liverpool		
	Full-time	Part-time[2]	Full-time	Part-time	
<3 (<15)	32.3 (23.4)	34.6 (25.9)	29.0 (16.7)	57.1 (33.3)	23.8 (30.8)
3-10 (16-35)	28.8 (42.0)	42.0 (40.7)	42.8 (50.7)	23.8 (42.9)	41.0 (43.2)
10-22 (35-59)	22.6 (26.5)	18.5 (14.8)	19.9 (28.3)	– (14.3)	17.0 (17.9)
22-48 (60-89)	11.2 (6.9)	2.5 (12.3)	4.0 (3.3)	4.8 (9.5)	10.9 (6.2)
>48 (>90)	5.2 (1.4)	1.2 (4.9)	4.3 (1.1)	14.3 (–)	7.3 (1.9)
Absolute total	393 (100)	81 (100)	276 (100)	21 (100)	3826 (100)
C^1	0.24 (0.21)		0.23 (0.40)		

Notes: 1.   Contingency coefficient.
2.   Includes part-time staff engaged for less than 10 hrs. per week (see Table 3.2).
3.   Part-time staff comprise such a small proportion of the total respondents at Reading, Swindon and Southampton that it is not considered useful to give the results.

Source: Office Survey, 1976

97

Reading, Swindon and Liverpool. For the offices in Southampton the difference is much narrower but the travel concessions available to employees in office 98 undoubtedly distorts the expected result.

THE ROLE OF OTHER VARIABLES

It has been suggested earlier that the ratio of full to part-time office staff could influence the distribution of trip time and distances for the journey to work in the study towns. Part-time office staff, most of whom work 10-30 hours per week, will probably seek employment which curtails the amount of travelling time to a minimum in order to reduce the uncertainty of fulfilling other commitments such as collecting children from school or getting from schools to workplaces on time in the morning for example. This consideration is likely to be particularly important for part-time staff who are not involved in flexible working hours. Part-time employees will also earn proportionally less than full-time office workers and will therefore be anxious to reduce travel costs accordingly. There were only two centres where part-time staff comprised a large enough proportion of the sample to be able to compare their journey to work characteristics with those of full-time staff (Table 5.6). At Watford, where the offices have the largest proportion of part-time staff, 77 percent of them travel less than 10km compared with 61 percent of the full-time office staff; the equivalent figures for Liverpool are 81 percent and 71 percent respectively. For the distance variable the values of C are almost identical for both sets of data and suggest a relatively weak association between travel distance and full/part-time status. The results are rather better for trip time, especially for the Liverpool sample where C has a value of 0.40. But the value of C for trip time at Watford is lower than that for trip distance. Therefore it is not possible, perhaps in view of the small sample available here, to conclude that part-time office workers have journeys to work which are significantly different from full-time office workers.

It is not intended to discuss the relationship between travel mode choice and trip time/distance for the journey to work in detail in this chapter but two variables relevant to the analysis in Chapter 6 are car ownership of office worker households and the ability of respondents to drive a car/van. These variables are introduced here because they are closely associated with trip distance (Table 5.7). The association is stronger than that with journey time with values of C for the former approaching 0.30 for car ownership in all centres except Watford where it reaches

Table 5.7

Contingency coefficients for the relationship between trip time/trip distance for the journey to work and car ownership and ability to drive a car – offices in survey towns

Car ownership and ability to drive a car	Survey towns									
	Watford		Reading		Swindon		Southampton		Liverpool	
	N^1	C^2	N	C	N	C	N	C	N	C
Car ownership/trip time	417	0.15	1240	0.09	980	0.11	540	0.16	273	0.17
Car ownership/trip distance	417	0.35	1239	0.26	986	0.23	540	0.29	273	0.27
Able to drive/trip time	431	0.22	1286	0.10	1019	0.08	572	0.12	277	0.14
Able to drive/trip distance	431	0.26	1266	0.23	1026	0.24	572	0.24	277	0.33

Notes: 1. Number of respondents providing data for both variables.

2. Contingency coefficient.

Source: Office Survey, 1976.

0.35. The fact that employees from households which own one or more cars are more likely to travel further than non-car owning households does not mean that private transport is actually used but it obviously increases the likelihood that the mode choice distributions discussed in Chapter 6 will be related to this situation. The association between journey times and household car ownership is weaker with values of C not exceeding 0.17 (Liverpool). Employees travelling from car-owning households may not be able to drive a car, or a vehicle may not be available for them to use, and public transport must then be substituted with negative consequences for the journey times of many of the employees affected.

A similar dichotomy exists in relation to the ability to drive a car (Table 5.7). In many cases this variable is a surrogate, as is car ownership, for occupation status and similar variables. Since we already know that higher income groups travel furthest on average and are more likely to own at least one car it is to be expected that ability to drive is positively related to trip distance with a maximum of 0.33 for the Liverpool offices and 0.23 the minimum (Reading). Again the relationship with trip time for the journey to work is weak for most centres. This is caused by the discrepancy between household car ownership and method of travel to work (see Appendix). Reading has the lowest scores for C for both variables and this probably arises from its more varied social and residential structure and that of its surrounding area.

All five centres have at least some office staff employed on the basis of flexible working hours although the proportion does vary considerably (Table 5.8). In Reading almost all the respondents work flexible hours but in Southampton, Liverpool and Swindon there is a more balanced distribution while in Watford the majority are not involved with flexible hours. These provide a suitable range of circumstances to confirm the uncertainty expressed in the Follow-Up Survey about the journey to work benefits enjoyed by employees able to choose the time when they travel to their offices and so avoid peak hour congestion.[9] The results for the offices in the Follow-Up Survey were inconclusive but it is now possible, using the data for the five centres, to be more positive. The distribution of trip times for 'flexible' and 'non-flexible' employees, along with the low values of C in all cases would seem to indicate that there are only marginal trip time advantages to be gained as a result of working flexible hours. Indeed, closer scrutiny of Table 5.7 shows that the proportion of trips lasting less than 35 minutes in the town where flexible working

Table 5.8

Contrasts in trip time distribution for office employees working
flexible hours – survey towns

Trip time (mins)	Watford		Reading		Survey towns Swindon		Southampton		Liverpool	
	F	NF	F	NF	F	NF	F	NF	F	NF
< 15	32.8	22.9	15.1	23.2	36.8	46.7	18.1	17.0	21.2	16.7
16–35	42.6	41.0	53.0	46.3	54.4	43.3	52.9	48.3	53.0	49.4
36–59	21.3	25.2	20.9	23.2	8.5	6.9	20.0	25.1	24.2	27.9
60–89	1.6	9.0	8.6	5.3	–	1.4	3.8	5.7	1.5	4.3
> 90	1.6	1.9	2.4	1.9	0.3	1.7	5.2	3.9	–	0.4
Absolute total	61	424	1175	195	307	767	210	409	66	233
C^1	0.12		0.13		0.16		0.13		0.31	

Notes: 1.   Contingency coefficient.

2.   Employees on flexible hours.

Source: Office Survey, 1976.

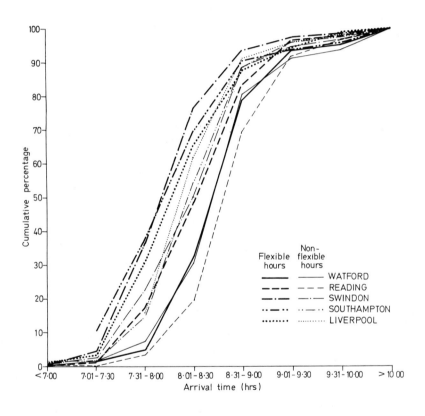

Figure 5.3   Arrival times of office staff in survey towns
             according to flexible/non-flexible working
             hours.

predominates, Reading, is only just lower for flexible office staff at 68/69 percent respectively. It seems reasonable to expect that the difference would be larger. This does occur where workers on flexible hours are in the minority with 75/64 percent at Watford, 71/65 percent at Southampton and 74/66 percent at Liverpool. Office employees who are working flexible hours clearly have shorter journey times in these three centres but this only produces a significant improvement in the value of C at Liverpool (0.31). Could it be, therefore, that in places where flexible working is the exception rather than the rule, office staff actually involved have better opportunity to benefit in journey to work terms because the majority of the workforce must still travel during the 'normal' hours? In Reading, on the other hand where there are so many office staff working flexible hours, (assuming that there are other office workers also involved) any spread effect on peak hour travel demand is counter-acted by the numbers involved and trip times are not enhanced in a similar way to those at Liverpool or Watford.

It is interesting that the limited improvements in the journey to work times of employees working flexible hours in Reading should coincide with arrival time curves for each group of office workers which are clearly distinctive (Fig. 5.3). The arrival times of employees at each office have been calculated by adding total journey times for the present journey to work to the time of departure from home on the day of the survey (see Appendix). Almost 50 percent of the office workers on flexiole hours at Reading arrive at their offices before 0830 hours compared with only 19 percent of their non-flexible colleagues. For Swindon the equivalent statistics are 76.4 percent and 50 percent. Where flexible hours are only utilized by a limited number of workers the difference between arrival time curves for each group is less well defined although flexible workers still tend to arrive earlier. The exception is clearly Watford where the two curves are almost identical and the value of C (0.08) is negligible. Elsewhere arrival time is clearly influenced by flexible/non-flexible working with C ranging between 0.30 (Reading) to 0.45 (Liverpool). We would expect this relationship to produce lower journey times on average for the majority who travel off-peak or during the early part of the peak period in Reading; it seems that so many office workers are doing so that congestion costs are being spread over a wider period and flexible hours are self defeating. This must be a tentative conclusion, however, because data from a better structured and more comprehensive sample needs to be collated in order to verify conclusions based on the rather selective data used here. It would be useful, for

Table 5.9

Incidence of waiting time during the journey to work in relation to total trip time

Survey town	Waiting Time (%)	Total trip time (mins)					Total trips	C^1
		<15	16-36	36-59	60-89	>90		
WATFORD	No Wait	99.1[2]	70.5	55.8	30.8	33.3*	339	0.44
	>16%	0.9	17.0	20.0	43.5	33.3	78	
READING	No Wait	91.4	65.8	45.0	23.2	48.4	849	0.38
	>16%	5.4	15.5	17.9	29.5	19.3	214	
SWINDON	No Wait	98.1	74.1	45.6	63.6	50.0	883	0.41
	>16%	1.0	14.8	24.0	18.2	21.4	103	
SOUTHAMPTON	No Wait	96.3	70.1	32.4	35.5	36.4	390	0.45
	>16%	2.8	14.1	25.5	22.6	22.7	96	
LIVERPOOL	No Wait	94.3	56.0	43.2	36.4	66.7*	175	0.41
	>16%	5.7	25.3	30.8	27.3	–	69	

Notes: 1.   Contingency coefficient.

2.   Percentage of total trips in each time group.

3.   * denotes categories represneted by less than 10 trips

Source: Office Survey, 1976.

example, to match employees with similar journey distances and travel modes but travelling to or from work at different times of the day.

The total travel time for any employee's journey to work usually includes an element of time spent waiting for connections. Within the limitations already mentioned in the introduction to this chapter it seems clear that the proportion of waiting time increases as the total time taken for the journey to work increases (Table 5.9). For the two centres nearest London, Watford and Reading waiting time which represents 16 percent or more of total journey time increases in each higher time category with the highest values in the 60-89 minute group. In all, some 25-30 percent of the respondents have to devote more than 16 percent of their total journey time to waiting for their conveyances to arrive. The values of C for each centre (0.38-0.45) confirm that there is a strong association between journey time and waiting time irrespective of location although the absolute amount of waiting time incurred in each centre will depend upon the modal structure of work trips and the relationship between these two variables will be considered in the next chapter.

DETERMINANTS OF INDIVIDUAL JOURNEY TO WORK TIMES AND DISTANCES

The discussion so far has concentrated on the aggregate travel to work characteristics of office workers and various sub-groups within and between centres. It has been demonstrated that the occupation status or the sex of an office worker can be used with some confidence to predict their journey to work profiles. However, the reliance on cross-tabulation (mainly two-way), contingency tests, the coefficient of variability and the contingency coefficient leaves considerable uncertainty about the relative importance of the variables used in the analysis thus far. How important are they for explaining the journey to work of individual office workers?

Some of this uncertainty can be eliminated by using stepwise multiple regression to identify a linear combination of independent variables which correlate as highly as possible with a dependent variable. The technique involves searching for the best prediction of the dependent variable with the fewest independent variables. Four dependent variables will be considered here: trip time and trip distance for the present journey to work of individual office workers and the changes, compared with trip times and trip distances

Table 5.10
Multiple regression analysis for office worker journey to
work trip times in survey towns

Dependent variable Y	Independent variables[1]					N
	X_1	X_2	X_3	X_4	X_5	
TRIP TIME (LOG)						
WATFORD	13	10	8	2	9	341
Multiple r	0.634	0.703	0.718	0.720	0.721	
r^2	0.402	0.494	0.151	0.519	0.520	
READING	13	19	2	4	11	949
Multiple r	0.661	0.707	0.710	0.712	0.714	
r^2	0.436	0.499	0.504	0.507	0.509	
SWINDON	13	19	2	10	7	715
Multiple r	0.369	0.500	0.517	0.524	0.528	
r^2	0.136	0.251	0.268	0.275	0.280	
SOUTHAMPTON	13	19	10	12	9	435
Multiple r	0.556	0.617	0.628	0.631	0.633	
r^2	0.309	0.381	0.394	0.399	0.401	
LIVERPOOL	13	10	11	2	8	193
Multiple r	0.475	0.572	0.588	0.597	0.600	
r^2	0.226	0.328	0.346	0.357	0.360	

Note: 1.   Independent variables are as follows:

Sex (2)   Car sharing (10)
Age (4)   Flexible hours (11)
Previous place of employment (7)   Occupation status (12)
Ability to dirve car (8)   Trip distance (Log) (13)
Car ownership (9)   Travel mode (19)

Source: Office Survey, 1976.

to previous workplaces, which these journeys represent. Nineteen independent variables have been used as the basis for identifying the five variables which contribute most to explaining the variation in the values of each of the dependent variables.[10]   The principal criterion for selecting independent variables is that they should have a strong association with the dependent variable but a weak association with each other. This ensures that the variation in the dependent variable is not explained by independent variables which may be surrogates for each other. It is, of course, difficult to entirely eliminate this problem when using variables such as sex and occupation status, for example, since they are not truly independent of each other. A second consideration is whether the values for each variable are normally distributed.   This is certainly not the case for the continuous data such as trip time and distance and these have therefore been transformed by calculating the log of the appropriate values for each employee to produce a more normal distribution.[11]

The relationship between trip time as the dependent variable in each centre and the selected independent variables is shown in Table 5.10 in which the latter are listed in the order in which they have been entered into the regression equation.   The proportion of the variation in the dependent variable explained by the first independent variable and the addition of each subsequent variable is given by the coefficient of determination (r^2).   In general the largest improvements in r^2 occur as a result of introducing the second and third variables, subsequent additions do not create substantial improvements in the proportion of the variation explained. A total of ten different independent variables is included in the results for all five centres with the trip distance (13) always the first variable to be forced into the equation. There are large differences, however, in the contribution of this variable to explaining the variability in trip times for the journey to work. In Watford and Reading, which have centralized office location distributions, trip distance accounts for 40-44 percent of the variation in employee trip times but only for 14 and 23 percent at Swindon and Liverpool which have a more dispersed distribution of office buildings in the sample. Southampton with 31 percent, is in an intermediate position which may also reflect its classification as a centre with an intermediate distribution of office premises.

A further 10 percent of the variation in trip time is explained by the mode of travel used (Reading, Swindon and Southampton) and by the incidence of car sharing (Watford and Liverpool).   There is a positive correlation of 0.11 and 0.30 between the latter variable and trip time in Watford and Liverpool respectively

Table 5.11
Multiple regression analysis for office worker journey to
work distances in survey towns

| Dependent variable Y | Independent variables[1] | | | | | N |
	X_1	X_2	X_3	X_4	X_5	
TRIP DISTANCE (LOG)						
WATFORD	14	12	10	19	4	341
Multiple r	0.384	0.470	0.511	0.517	0.519	
r^2	0.147	0.221	0.262	0.267	0.270	
READING	2	12	19	10	9	949
Multiple r	0.317	0.341	0.366	0.412	0.431	
r^2	0.100	0.117	0.134	0.170	0.186	
SWINDON	10	14	12	4	9	715
Multiple r	0.319	0.409	0.442	0.457	0.461	
r^2	0.101	0.168	0.195	0.209	0.212	
SOUTHAMPTON	14	2	10	19	12	
Multiple r	0.395	0.475	0.497	0.516	0.531	
r^2	0.156	0.226	0.247	0.266	0.282	
LIVERPOOL	14	12	19	11	9	193
Multiple r	0.481	0.558	0.577	0.601	0.608	
r^2	0.232	0.311	0.333	0.362	0.370	

Note: 1. Independent variables are as follows:

Sex (2)   Occupation status (12)
Age (4)   Previous trip distance (Log) (14)
Car ownership (9)   Travel mode (19)
Car sharing (10)
Flexible hours (11)

Source: Office Survey, 1976.

and this suggests that we can expect employees who share vehicles to spend less time on the journey to work. Similarly the values of r for travel mode and trip time in Reading, Swindon and Southampton respectively are 0.30, 0.23 and 0.25. These two variables are interchangeable since there is a correlation of 0.61 between travel mode and car sharing in Reading, for example, so that the incidence of car sharing in each centre may determine which of the two variables will be included in the equation. Hence, in total, some 50 percent of the variation in trip times at Watford and Reading are accounted for by the distance travelled to work and either travel mode or car sharing. The level of explanation is considerably lower in the other centres and this continues to be the case after subsequent independent variables have been added. At Swindon and Reading the sex of a respondent reduces the explanation of trip time variation by a further 1 percent which is rather less than the 1-2 percent improvement at Watford (ability to drive a car), Southampton (car sharing) and Liverpool (flexible hours). Most of the remaining variables included in the regression equations are connected with access to private transport and occupation status, for example, is only included (as the fourth independent variable) in the Southampton equation.

The distances travelled to offices by employees are less satisfactorily accounted for by the independent variables in the regression equation (Table 5.11). The first variable entered is not the same for every centre although previous distance travelled to work is entered first in three of the equations but only explains between 15 percent (Watford) and 23 percent (Liverpool) of the variation in present trip distance. These are the centres where central London recruits are the least important sub-samples, thus leaving scope for a stronger association between present and previous journey to work distances. For the Reading sample the sex of office workers is the first variable to be entered but only generates an r^2 of 10 percent while car sharing, which has a negative correlation of -0.32 with trip distance, accounts for a similar proportion of the variation for Swindon office staff.

The addition of further variables helps to explain a further 10-15 percent of the variation in trip distances with occupation status entering as the second variable in the Watford, Reading and Liverpool equations. This creates substantial improvements in r^2 in two instances but only to a marginal change from 10 to 12 percent at Reading. Occupation status is also the third variable to be entered in the Swindon equation but is only the fifth item to be included at Southampton. The overall level of explanation for trip distance

Table 5.12
Multiple regression analysis for office worker journey to work
change (distance travelled) in survey towns

Dependent variable Y	Independent variables[1]					N
	X_1	X_2	X_3	X_4	X_5	
TRIP DISTANCE CHANGE						
WATFORD	14	12	20	2	10	341
Multiple r	0.466	0.501	0.509	0.514	0.517	
r^2	0.217	0.251	0.259	0.264	0.268	
READING	14	2	12	19	10	949
Multiple r	0.695	0.717	0.722	0.726	0.731	
r^2	0.483	0.514	0.522	0.527	0.534	
SWINDON	14	2	20	12	10	715
Multiple r	0.700	0.712	0.716	0.719	0.721	
r^2	0.491	0.506	0.513	0.518	0.520	
SOUTHAMPTON	14	12	2	7	11	435
Multiple r	0.699	0.721	0.728	0.733	0.737	
r^2	0.488	0.520	0.530	0.537	0.543	
LIVERPOOL	14	12	7	9	20	193
Multiple r	0.522	0.576	0.596	0.611	0.612	
r^2	0.305	0.332	0.355	0.373	0.375	

Note: 1. Independent variables are as follows:

Sex (2)   Flexible hours (11)
Previous place of employment (7) Occupation status (12)
Car ownership (9)   Previous trip distance (log) (14)
Car sharing (10)   Present travel mode (19)
                                         Previous travel mode (20)

Source: Office Survey, 1976.

variation remains low, however, compared with trip time although the independent variables entered into the regression equation are fewer in number, i.e. previous trip distance, occupation status, travel mode and car sharing. The lowest overall r^2 for five independent variables is returned for Reading (0.186), closely followed by Swindon (0.212) which may be an indication that the size and diversity of office industries in the sample may be more important determinants of the spatial distribution and therefore distances travelled to work by office workers.

Finally, the difference between the present and previous journey to work attributes of individual workers may also be connected with particular independent variables. Equations were therefore calculated for trip time differences and trip distance difference and for the former the values of r^2 are low and the five variables explain less than 10 percent of the difference between present and previous trip times. The principal exception is Reading where the overall order of explanation is similar to that achieved for journey to work distances. Trip distance difference is the first variable entered into the regression equation and generates an r^2 of 0.157 and this increases to 0.169 (travel mode) and subsequently to 0.178 (previous place of work).

The prediction of trip length change is generally superior (Table 5.12) and Watford is the only centre with an initial r^2 for the first variable entered below 22 percent. In every case the principal determinant of trip distance difference is the distance travelled to previous place of employment. Employees with very long journeys to work prior to decentralization are now able to live much closer to their workplaces and in those centres with large numbers of central London staff (Reading, Swindon and Southampton) almost 50 percent of the variation in trip distance changes is explained by the independent variable. Subsequent improvements in r^2 are much smaller, however, than they are for the trip time equation but similar variables dominate the next two places in the regression equations. These are occupation status (Southampton, Liverpool and Watford) and the sex of respondents (Reading and Swindon) as second order independent variables, followed by previous mode of travel (Watford and Swindon) and either occupation status (Reading), sex (Southampton) or previous place of work as the third order variables. Therefore, just five variables account for a large proportion of the variation in trip distance changes for the journey to work of office staff in all five study centres.

NOTES AND REFERENCES

(1)   Since the survey was undertaken in Southampton
      the bridge over the R. Test, which has been
      recently opened, has improved the accessibility
      of the city centre from the east, particularly
      with reference to the distance travelled to
      work.

(2)   The number of stages which comprise individual
      work journeys are discussed more fully in Chapter
      6.

(3)   Most journey to work studies draw attention to
      the contrasts in male/female travel characteristics,
      some examples include J.S. Wabe, 'Dispersal
      of employment and the journey to work', Journal
      of Transport Economics and Policy, Vol. 1,
      1967, pp. 345-61; E.J. Taafe et.al., The Peripheral
      Journey to Work: A Geographic Consideration,
      North Western University Press, Evanston 1963;
      J.F. Kain, 'The journey to work as a determinant
      of residential location', Papers and Proceedings
      of the Regional Science Association, Vol. 9,
      1965, pp. 137-60; L.K. Loewenstein, The Location
      of Residences and Workplaces in Urban Areas,
      Scarecrow Press, New York 1965; A. Hecht, 'The
      journey to work distance in relation to the
      socio-economic characteristics of workers',
      Canadian Geographer, Vol. 18, 1974, pp. 367-
      78; H.F. Andrews, 'Journey to work considerations
      in the labour force participation of married
      women', Regional Studies, Vol. 12, 1978, pp.
      11-20.

(4)   This is also shown by the data in the Follow-
      Up Survey, see P.W. Daniels, A Follow-Up Study
      of the Journey to Work at Decentralized Offices
      in Britain: Final Report (Part I), Departments
      of Environment and Transport, London 1978,
      paras. 4.11-4.13.

(5)   Also illustrated in the Follow-Up Survey, see
      P.W. Daniels, A Follow-Up of the Journey to
      Work at Decentralized Offices in Britain: Final
      Report (Part II), Case Studies at New Malden,
      Southampton, Leicester and Durham, Departments
      of Environment and Transport, London 1978,
      Fig. 9.2.

(6)   For equivalent statistics in Follow-Up Survey
      see P.W. Daniels, op.cit., 1978, (Parts I and
      II).

(7) Ibid., (Part I), Appendix B, Table 8.

(8) The coefficient of variability provides a measure
     of the relative homogeneity of groups which
     have different means and standard deviations.
     The size of the standard deviation relative
     to the mean is measured where:

$$V = \frac{s}{\bar{x}}$$

     If V is less than 1.0 it indicates that s is
     less than the mean (which is usually to be
     expected). The range of V values for each
     sub-group then provides an indication of whether
     or not they are homogeneous. See H.M. Blalock,
     Social Statistics, McGraw Hill, New York 1960.

(9) P.W. Daniels, op.cit., 1978 (Part I), paras.
     5.36-5.38.

(10) The list of variables included in the stepwise
     regression equation is as follows:

          Difference between previous and present journey
            time (1)
          Sex (2)
          Marital status (3)
          Age (4)
          Present journey time (5)
          Previous journey time (6)
          Previous place of work (7)
          Ability to drive a car (present) (8)
          Car ownership (present) (9)
          Car sharing (10)
          Flexible hours (11)
          Present occupation (12)
          Present journey distance (13)
          Previous journey distance (14)
          Arrival time at office (15)
          Difference between previous and present journey
            distance (16)
          Waiting time (present) (17)
          Waiting time (previous) (18)
          Travel mode (present) (19)
          Travel mode (previous) (20)

(11) A skewed distribution of trip distances and times
     for the journey to work is also clearly illustrated
     in P.W. Daniels, op.cit., 1978 (Part I), Figs.
     5.5 and 5.6.

6 Modes of travel for the journey to work of office staff

CAR OWNERSHIP AND MODAL CHOICE

Some reference has already been made to car ownership
in the context of the distances travelled to work
but the actual distribution of car ownership in the
sample has not yet been considered (see chapter 5).
It may be useful, therefore, to open this chapter
with some details about car ownership by sex in the
study towns as a prerequisite for understanding some
of the modal characteristics of the journey to work
trips generated by the decentralized offices.

With a larger proportion of managerial and professional
office staff in this sample by comparison with the
Follow-Up Survey, it is not surprising to find that
there are even more office workers in the survey towns
who travel from households with at least one car (Table
6.1). Over 20 percent of the office workers in the
Follow-Up Survey travelled to work from households
which did not possess a car but in the survey towns
the equivalent figure is less than 15 percent. The
proportion of respondents from households with one
car is identical in both sets of data (61.2 percent),
leaving households with two or more cars to account
for 24 percent of the office workers in the survey
towns. Thus, almost 1 in 4 of all households have
two or more cars compared with less than 1 in 5 in
the Follow-Up Survey. When the overall totals are
disaggregated by sex for each centre there is a consistent
distinction between the proportion of car-owning households in each group. Less than 15 percent of male
office workers are from non-car owning households
compared with approximately 17 percent of females
in four of the centres. The exception is Liverpool
where 35 percent of the females are from non-car owning
households. Reading and Swindon have the largest
proportions of one-car households for both male and
female office workers but only the female respondents
at Watford travel from an above-average proportion
of two-car households. Watford also has the lowest
level of one-car households amongst male respondents
(50 percent) and the highest level of two-car households
(35 percent). In Reading and Swindon there is only
a marginal difference in the latter proportion for
males and females. Comparison of these results with
the household car ownership statistics from the 1971
Census shows that office workers in all the centres
are more likely to be car owners than the population
as a whole.[1]

Table 6.1

Household car ownership and ability to drive a car — by sex

Car Ownership	Watford		Reading		Survey Towns Swindon		Southampton		Liverpool		Overall Total		Follow-Up Survey
	M	F	M	F	M	F	M	F	M	F			
No car	14.9	15.7	9.9	18.5	9.4	13.3	13.6	17.2	13.8	35.0	503	14.6	(20.3)
One car	50.5	56.2	65.5	59.5	64.4	65.2	57.7	47.2	49.2	55.4	2100	61.2	(61.2)
Two+ cars	34.7	28.1	24.7	22.1	26.1	21.5	28.7	17.4	27.6	9.6	833	24.3	(18.5)
Able to drive (%)[1]	91.8	56.4	92.6	58.4	88.2	55.3	88.6	54.2	83.9	40.9	77.2		
Absolute total[2]	202	210	791	444	416	563	279	253	116	157	3436	100	(100)
	(100)	(100)	(100)	(100)	(100)	(100)	(100)	(100)	(100)	(100)	(100)		

Note: 1.   The proportion is calculated for those office workers who answered the relevant question, not the car ownership question.

        2.   Non-respondents are excluded.

Sources: Office Survey, 1976.
           Follow-Up Survey, 1976.

In absolute terms, it therefore emerges that Reading and Swindon have considerably fewer respondents from households without a car than expected from the overall distribution for all five centres. The frequency of one-car households is above average whereas Watford and Southampton have fewer one-car households but two-car and non-car households are both over-represented. Both one- and two-car households are under-represented in the Liverpool sample while there is a far higher proportion than expected of office workers from households without a car. The car ownership profiles of the office workers in five centres therefore reveal significant variations which can be expected to generate contrasting choices of travel mode from the journey to work.

One other consideration which will affect travel mode choice is the ability of respondents to drive a car. Between 84 and 94 percent of the male office workers indicated that they were able to drive but, except for Liverpool (41 percent), only 54-62 percent of female respondents replied in the same way (Table 6.1).

The possible effect of the differential level of ability to drive a car on modal choice is clearly indicated in Fig. 6.1. Although there are variations in the proportion of bus journeys generated by the offices in each centre, the majority of these journeys are undertaken by female office staff (65-80 percent) especially in Watford, Southampton and Liverpool. Females who drive to work only acount for 20-25 percent of all car driver journeys but car passengers, on the other hand, are almost exclusively female. Male office staff are just as likely to walk to work as females in Watford, Reading and Southampton but this is not true for Liverpool and Swindon, especially the latter where 23 percent of the females walk to their offices. For most journeys to work by train, males are much more significant than females. Without any consideration at this point of the actual modal distribution of trips, it seems that the ratio of male to female office workers in an office building or separate organisations within it can provide a valuable indication of the likely demand for the various methods of travel available for journey to work trips. Indeed, there is a consistent association in all the survey towns between travel mode and sex (0.38 - 0.44) which gives added weight to the merits of this hypothesis.

If this hypothesis is correct we could expect to find that centres with a high male/female staff ratio will generate a larger proprotion of car driver trips than centres with a more equally balanced ratio or a low male/female ratio. The data, illustrated in

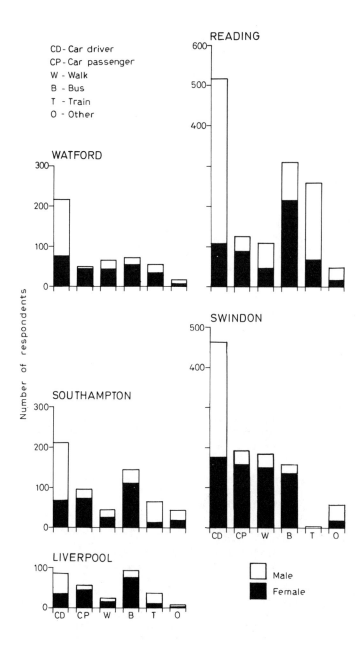

Figure 6.1 Travel mode by sex

117

Fig. 6.1, does corroborate the hypothesis to a limited degree. Car driver trips in Reading (1.6:1 males/females) account for 43 percent of the journeys to work but at Watford (1:1.2) car drivers still comprise 45 percent of the total trips. The figures of 39 percent in Southampton (1:1) and 29 percent at Liverpool (1:1.5) are more in accord with expectations but in Swindon, which has a similar ratio to Liverpool (1:1.5), the proportion of car drivers is the same (45 percent) as that for Reading. There are therefore other factors such as the locations of individual offices, accessibility at the premises by public transport, or occupation structure which modify the relationship between male/female ratio and travel mode structure and some of these will be considered later in this chapter.

There are only two centres with more car drivers than expected from the distribution for all five centres, Watford and Swindon. In the former the difference is 216/186 and 464/421 in the latter. The proportion of car passengers trips, using the evidence from the Follow-Up Survey, can be expected to increase at offices further from London and this is confirmed; trips in this category are over-represented amongst Swindon (199/147), Southampton and Liverpool journeys to work. Office workers who travel to work on foot are, generally under-represented, particularly in Reading (106/151), although at Watford and Swindon there are approximately twice as many trips on foot as expected (189/119) and this is probably a function of the proximity of adjacent residential areas. Perhaps contrary to expectations created by the Follow-Up Survey results, bus trips only occur at a lower level than expected in Watford and Swindon; trips using this mode occur with above average frequency in the Reading (309/280) and Southampton (146/126) samples while the difference in Liverpool is much larger (92/62). The influence of contrasting office location patterns and markedly different levels of access to rail services is clearly illustrated by the Reading and Swindon samples. Almost twice as many of the Reading office staff as expected (258/149) travel to work by train compared with only 2/117 in Swindon.

It will therefore be interesting to examine further the data on travel mode for selected individual offices later in this chapter. One thing which is emerging is that public transport is used by a larger proportion of the respondents in the survey towns (32 percent) than in the Follow-Up Survey (29 percent). It appears that public transport is regaining some of the ground which it should have lost if the trends in travel mode for the journey, indicated in the 1969 survey had been continuing. [2] The rate of recovery is much slower, however, than the earlier scale of transfers from public to private modes. Nevertheless, it should not be overlooked that there are still many more trips by car (drivers and passengers) than indicated by data for each centre given in the 1971 Census.[3]

The relationship, as measured by C, between travel mode choice in the journey to work and car ownership is not well developed at all five centres (Table 6.2). Both Liverpool and Reading office workers have values of C below 0.30 but they increase to 0.44-0.54 in the remaining centres. As expected from the importance of car driver trips, the Watford sample generates the highest value of C (0.54). Hence, between one-half and one-third of all the journeys to work by bus or on foot are generated by office workers from households which do not own or have access to a company car/van. With employees from two-car households generating only some 5-10 percent of the trips by public transport the majority of the remaining public transport journeys are undertaken by employees from one-car households, many of whom are female office workers. With the exception of Watford, non-car owners do not comprise a large proportion (less than 1 in 5) of the respondents who travel to work by train but employees from two-car households are much better represented and there is clearly an occupational dimension to modal choice and this will be considered later. For the two remaining modal categories used in this analysis, access to a car is almost a pre-requisite although 8.4 percent of the Liverpool office staff who drive to work claim not to have full use of, or access, to a car/van. Apart from Liverpool, it also seems that an office worker's chances of travelling to work as a car passenger (and by implication possible involvement in car sharing) is much reduced if he or she does not belong to a car owning household. Less than 7 percent of car passenger journeys are made by employees in this category although at Liverpool this factor does not appear to be a major consideration. Many car passengers, whether participating in car pools or not, must usually expect to be able to reciprocate This situation may now change, however, as a result of the recent relaxation on payments to car drivers for providing lifts to colleagues and others (1978 Transport Act) provided that the sum received is not more than the actual cost of undertaking each work trip.[4]

The ability to drive is closely associated with travel mode in all five centres (Table 6.2) with C ranging between 0.42 and 0.51. Bus users are least likely to be able to drive, especially in Southampton, Liverpool and Swindon.

Table 6.2

Travel mode by car ownership and ability to drive a car

Survey town	Car ownership and ability to drive a car	Travel mode						C^{1}
		Car driver	Car pass.	Walk	Bus	Train	Other	
Watford	No car	–	6.8	37.1	46.8	26.7	21.4	
	One car	52.8	70.5	41.9	42.6	55.6	64.3	0.54
	Two+ car	47.2	22.7	4.8	10.6	17.8	28.5	
	Able to drive (%)	96.2(213)[2]	42.2(45)	55.4(56)	50.9(53)	52.2(46)	70.6(17)	0.51
Reading	No car	1.4	2.5	36.6	31.2	12.5	22.7	
	One car	62.2	2.5	36.6	57.5	73.2	54.5	0.29
	Two+ cars	36.5	27.7	6.5	11.3	14.3	22.7	
	Able to drive (%)	98.2(510)	66.7(120)	68.1(94)	52.5(265)	84.7(229)	78.3(46)	0.44
Swindon	No car	0.9	9.8	27.6	30.0	–	24.6	
	One car	62.4	77.3	59.9	62.5	–	59.6	0.42
	Two+ cars	36.8	12.9	12.5	7.5	100.0	15.8	
	Able to drive (%)	96.3(464)	51.8(199)	36.5(189)	25.3(162)	100.0(2)	64.5(62)	0.53
Southampton	No car	1.9	5.3	50.0	40.6	21.1	28.9	
	One car	57.9	73.7	50.0	50.0	59.6	50.0	0.49
	Two+ cars	40.2	21.1	–	9.4	19.3	21.1	
	Able to drive (%)	96.7(210)	61.2(98)	60.0(35)	40.2(122)	78.1(64)	61.0(41)	0.47
Liverpool	No car	8.4	16.4	38.9	48.7	18.2	62.5	
	One car	54.2	76.4	61.1	44.7	66.7	12.5	0.25
	Two+ cars	37.3	27.1	–	6.6	15.2	25.0	
	Able to drive (%)	92.9(84)	58.2(55)	36.8(19)	24.7(77)	73.5(34)	37.5(8)	0.51

Notes: 1. Contingency coefficient.
2. Value in brackets is total number of respondents after excluding non-respondents.

Source: Office Survey, 1976.

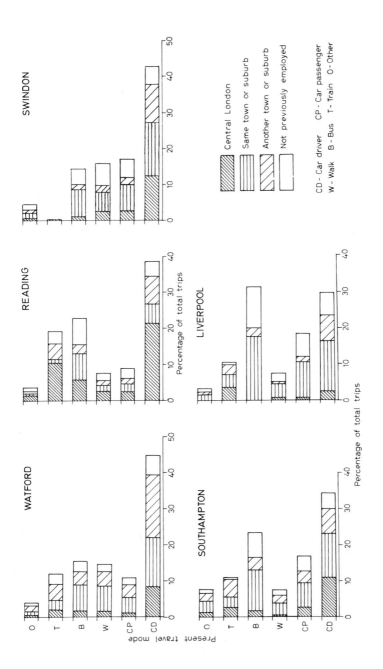

Figure 6.2   Modal choice and previous workplace

121

PREVIOUS WORKPLACE, OCCUPATION STATUS AND MODAL CHOICE

The importance of previous workplace as a determinant of modal choice for the journey to work is demonstrated in Fig. 6.2.[5] Almost without exception the rule seems to be that central London recruits will travel to work as car drivers or by train in proportions larger than their overall representation in the respective samples. Hence, 54 percent of the work journeys by train at Reading are made by former central London office workers who comprise 43 percent of all the respondents; the proportion driving to work is 56 percent. A similar generalisation can be made for recruits from other parts of the country with the minor exception of car drivers in Southampton. It is therefore inevitable that the utilisation of bus services in the study towns largely relies on the level of patronage by local recruits and office workers classified as not previously employed. In all five centres journeys to work by bus are the second most important group of trips and at least 35 percent, and in Liverpool 57 percent, of these trips are undertaken by local recruits. If the equivalent trips by new recruits to the labour force are included then in Liverpool 92 percent of all the journeys to work by bus are made by 'local' office staff; equivalent figures for the other centres are: Watford, 70 percent; Reading 64 percent; Swindon 59 percent and Southampton 79 percent. This lends further support to the view that the composition of the office labour force is a key factor in any attempt to predict the likely impact of new office development on the modal structure of the journey to work.

Another interesting feature is that recruits from elsewhere are more likely to walk to work than to travel by bus (Fig. 6.2). Walking trips are also undertaken at levels above their overall share of the respondents, by local recruits and it seems likely that for the former group at least, the relocated offices have provided an opportunity to shorten and/or make easier and cheaper their journey to work. On the other hand, trips to work on foot are generally the least important group of journeys in terms of their share of total trips with the exception of Swindon where a larger number of office workers travel to work on foot rather than travel by bus.

The correlation between occupation status and previous workplace has been clearly demonstrated in Chapter 3 and in the Follow-Up Survey.[6] Thus the tendency for managerial and professional office staff to travel to work by train or as car drivers at a level which is disproportionate to their presence in the overall sample for each centre is to be expected. (Fig. 6.3).[7]

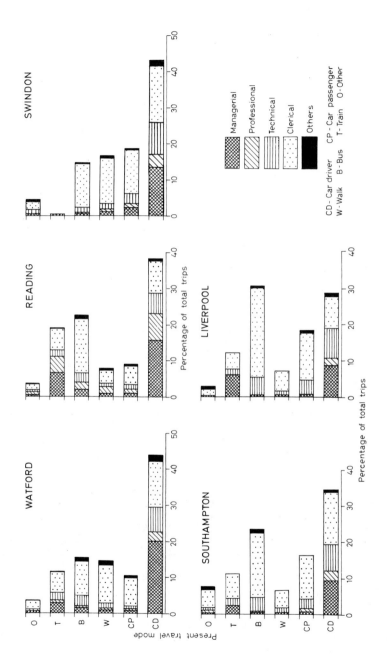

Figure 6.3 Modal choice and occupation status

The contingency coefficients show that there is a moderately close association between occupation status and travel mode; the value of 0.57 for Liverpool is to some extent misleading because of the absence of values for professional workers in several of the cells in the table. Between 62-80 percent of bus journeys are made by clerical workers even though in Reading they only represent 41 percent of the respondents. Employees who travel to work as car passengers are also most likely to be in the clerical group; an initial indication that car sharing will be dominated by local/clerical office staff whose social networks and spatial pattern of residences is more conducive to such arrangements than the more widely dispersed car-owning central London and other households.

TRIP DISTANCE AND TRAVEL MODE

Using a similar procedure to that already adopted for trip distances and sex by occupation status in Chapter 5, the mean distances travelled by male and female office workers using the alternative travel modes show a tendency towards heterogeneity rather than homogeneity (Table 6.3). Since most of the managers and professionals in the sample are male, and in the light of their travel mode decisions already outlined it is immediately apparent that male car drivers and train users travel considerably further than average in every centre except Reading where male employees who travel by train travel twice as far as car driving colleagues and raise the centre average (for male office staff) to 16.5 km which is the highest for the five centres. The values of V for car driver journeys show that a similar degree of variability in the distribution of origins exists for each town but this is not the case for train users who tend to travel similar distances so that all values of V are below 1.0. Bus and car passenger trips by male office staff show much more variability between centres; values of V above 2.0 occur for bus trips in Southampton and Reading, while also contributing to greater heterogeneity of trip distances by travel mode within each centre. In Reading the lowest value of V is 0.63 (train users) and the maximum 2.0 (bus users); at Southampton the range is 0.78 (walk) to 2.2 (bus users). The ranges of V are narrower in the three other centres and the mean trip distances for each modal category relate more closely to a 'general' pattern of trip origins in which walking journeys are at the core, followed outwards in successive distance zones by bus journeys, then car passenger/car driver journeys and an outer zone from which journeys to work by train are the principal method of travel.

Table 6.3

Mean trip distance by sex and travel mode

Sex and travel mode	Survey towns									
	Watford		Reading		Swindon		Southampton		Liverpool	
	$\bar{d}$	V^1	$\bar{d}$	V	$\bar{d}$	V	$\bar{d}$	V	$\bar{d}$	V
MALES	$(214)^2$ 15.2	1.257	(819) 16.5	1.133	(425) 10.2	1.673	(298) 13.4	1.369	(114) 11.8	1.159
Car driver	18.1	1.180	14.5	1.150	11.5	1.542	14.1	1.363	14.6	1.146
Car pass.	19.0 *	0.824	20.2	1.087	12.7	1.463	12.3	1.446	10.2	0.773
Walk	1.6	1.300	2.3	1.083	2.5	1.861	3.1	0.784	5.1 *	0.092
Bus	9.4	0.906	5.4	2.002	4.9	1.859	7.3	2.211	4.8	0.765
Train	17.5	0.907	30.4	0.633	5.0	–	22.6	0.901	13.7	0.983
FEMALES	(257) 7.6	1.552	(504) 8.0	1.311	(641) 4.5	1.803	(304) 5.7	1.191	(177) 6.8	1.680
Car driver	8.0	0.956	9.0	0.920	6.8	1.385	6.0	0.689	7.0	0.896
Car pass.	8.0	1.014	9.0	1.153	4.7	1.356	6.5	0.716	7.3	1.674
Walk	4.1	1.021	1.7	1.048	2.5	2.612	11.7	1.133	1.9	1.068
Bus	6.4	2.132	5.3	1.555	3.9	1.457	4.1	0.523	7.2	1.920
Train	14.0	0.992	19.4	0.804	–	–	20.7	1.124	11.6	0.770
Total population	11.0	1.447	13.2	1.251	6.8	1.885	9.5	1.504	8.7	1.435

Notes: 1. Coefficient of variability (s.d./$\bar{d}$)

2. Number of observations

* Denotes < 10 observations.

Source: Office Survey, 1976

125

Inter-centre variability for female journey to work distances by almost all the modes used is the rule while intra-centre homogeneity is also apparent (see Table 6.3). Bus trips by female office staff clearly have a wide range of origins with V reaching 2.1 in Watford. On the other hand, almost all the journeys by this group are below the overall average except journeys to work by train. Those females who drive to work will, in common with male colleagues, drive further than those who use bus services but only twice as far rather than 2-3 times as far in the case of males. The average distance for female car passenger journeys is marginally higher than for car drivers and this is an indication of the valuable role of this method of travel as a way of spreading and lowering costs in a way which allows workers to obtain employment at locations which would normally be out of reach for many of them, especially females.

The details given in Table 6.3 are summarised in Fig. 6.4 which shows the proportion of trip origins from each distance zone which can be assigned to each of the six travel modes used in this analysis. Journeys to work by bus and trips on foot predominate from origins within 3km of offices in these centres with car drivers accounting for a large proportion of the remaining journeys and providing a reason for the high values of V mentioned earlier. As distance travelled increases the share of car driver trips in each distance zone increases, along with the proportion of office staff who travel to work by train. Bus journeys decline sharply with distance and make up less than 10 percent of the origins in the 10-22km zone. The share of car driver origins declines beyond 48 km from which areas train journeys comprise more than 50 percent of work journeys although the absolute number of trips involved is small.

This pattern is most clearly represented by the Reading data but it is less clear for the other centres. There is certainly an element of uniformity in the share of car passenger and other modes in each distance zone at all five centres, but at a higher level of 10-20 percent in each case except Reading. At this point the similarity ends, however, and the shape of the curves for each of the travel modes is rather more variable. Nevertheless the decline in bus journeys beyond 22 km is again apparent and at Watford car driver journeys comprise more than 60 percent of all journeys to work beyond 22km compared with 45-55 percent at Southampton and Liverpool. Local travel conditions, the availability of competing travel modes and the pattern of office development undoubtedly affects the distributions illustrated in Fig. 6.4. The influence of office location patterns will be returned to in the last section of this chapter.

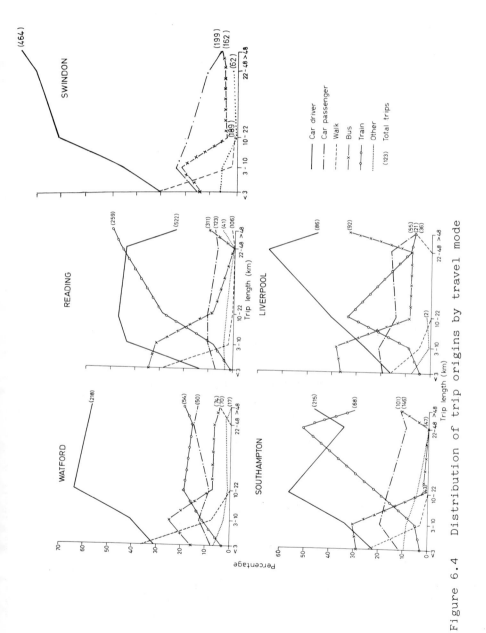

Figure 6.4   Distribution of trip origins by travel mode

Table 6.4

Mean trip times by sex and travel mode

Sex and mode	Watford $\bar{t}$	Watford V^1	Reading $\bar{t}$	Reading V	Survey towns Swindon $\bar{t}$	Swindon V	Southampton $\bar{t}$	Southampton V	Liverpool $\bar{t}$	Liverpool V
MALES	$(215)^2$ 33.6	0.719	(836) 34.9	0.752	(431) 21.2	0.900	(302) 36.0	0.929	(119) 32.4	0.547
Car Driver	33.0	0.734	28.6	0.641	21.0	0.871	33.0	1.273	28.3	0.480
Car Pass.	37.7 *	0.599	40.7	1.523	21.5	0.609	30.8	0.670	27.7	0.545
Walk	15.2	0.714	21.3	0.424	19.5	0.968	27.9	0.532	23.0 *	0.484
Bus	52.3	0.486	29.4	0.344	26.6	0.413	38.1	0.561	55.6	0.423
Train	47.9	0.279	55.0	0.509	149.0 *	0.238	49.1	0.397	45.6	0.490
FEMALES	(260) 30.4	0.640	(528) 30.8	0.582	(637) 21.0	0.690	(308) 30.5	0.671	(179) 29.5	0.519
Car Driver	25.8	0.683	27.8	0.548	19.0	0.658	24.0	0.476	27.7	0.543
Car Pass.	23.0	0.545	24.2	0.542	16.8	0.689	25.8	0.727	22.8	0.726
Walk	21.2	0.636	22.5	0.969	17.1	0.622	22.5	1.195	21.6	0.343
Bus	41.7	0.486	33.7	0.540	31.1	0.470	36.9	0.566	34.5	0.391
Train	45.9	0.431	43.5	0.391	–	–	39.5	0.494	42.8	0.366
Total population	31.9	0.683	33.3	0.704	21.1	0.782	33.2	0.836	30.6	0.533

Notes:

1. Coefficient of variability (s.d./$\bar{t}$).

2. Number of observations.

* Denotes < 10 observations.

Source: Office Survey, 1976

Mean trip times and travel mode

There is a greater degree of homogeneity in the data
for mean trip times by travel mode for both males
and females (Table 6.4). There are only two values
of V greater than 1.0 and both the inter- and intra-
centre ranges are much closer than the equivalent
data for journey to work distances. It is also clear
that there is less variability in public transport
journey times with V as low as 0.24 and 0.28 for males
travelling by train to the Watford and Swindon offices.
Bus users have rather higher values of V but lower
than most of the values for private transport users.
There are generally only minor differences between
V values for males and females using the same method
of travel and this is certainly not the case for trip
distances. Table 6.4 also shows that public transport
users have mean trip times which are almost always
higher than for private transport users. The former
seem particularly adverse in Watford where the mean
times for male and female bus trips are 52 minutes
and 42 minutes respectively, compared with 33 minutes
and 26 minutes for car drivers. The differences are
less extreme in the other centres but, in general
car drivers can be expected to spend 5-10 minutes
less travelling to the office than bus or train users
in spite of the differences in the trip distance curves
shown in Fig. 6.4.

Travel mode changes

While it was not the principal concern of this part
of the project to analyse the changes in the journey
to work which have contributed to journey to work
characteristics observed in each study town in 1976,
it may be useful to digress briefly to see whether
the transfer from public to private transport consequent
upon office employment relocation and typical of the
Follow-Up Survey offices, has also occurred in this
survey. The bar graphs in Fig. 6.5 (elaborated in
a slightly different way in Table 6.5) show the overall
structure of travel in each centre and the proportion
of trips by each modal category which can be attributed
to those office staff already using the same method
of travel as for their previous journey to work and
those which reflect the contribution of users who
have transferred from other modes. Hence, at Watford
some 45 percent of all work journeys are made by car
drivers and of these some 55 percent previously travelled
elsewhere as car drivers, 8 percent were previously
bus users and 19 percent previously travelled to work
by train. It is therefore possible to identify the
principal sources of any 'new' trips in each of the
modal categories at each centre. Since this information
can only be estimated from Fig. 6.5, more substantive

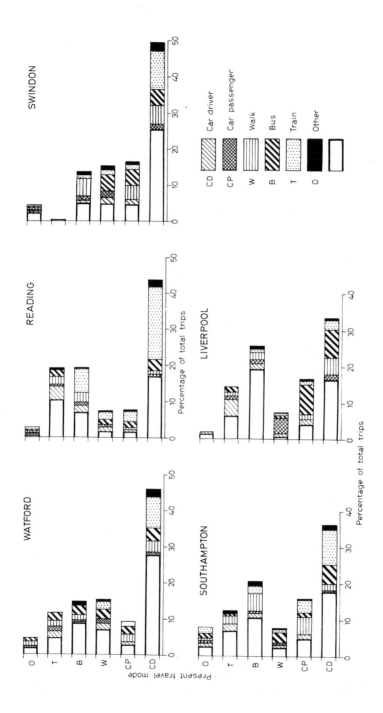

Figure 6.5 Travel mode transfers by office workers in the survey towns.

Table 6.5

Changes in travel mode for the journey to work to office in survey towns

Survey town	Travel mode	Travel mode changes					Principal previous modes	C^1
		A*	B	C	D	E^2		
WATFORD	Car D.	45.9³	32.9³	+49	83.9	69	Bus (7.5), Train (18.5)	
	Car P.	9.0	6.4	+10	37.5	25	Walk (23.5),Bus (23.5)	
	Walk	15.1	15.9	- 3	43.3	31	Bus (17.5), Train (15.8)	0.76
	Bus	14.3	20.4	-23	42.9	21	Walk (11.1), Train (16.7)	
	Train	11.4	19.1	-29	22.2	27	Car D. (16.3), Bus (20.9)	
READING	Car D.	43.5	24.9	+192	67.4	276	Bus (6.7), Train (48.0)	
	Car P.	7.6	4.1	+37	35.7	64	Bus (22.8), Train (35.4)	
	Walk	7.5	7.9	- 4	20.7	61	Car D. (16.7), Train (28.2)	0.50
	Bus	19.2	14.7	+47	48.0	126	Walk (13.7), Train (32.7)	
	Train	19.2	43.4	-250	23.8	92	Car D. (19.6), Walk (10.6)	
SWINDON	Car D.	49.0	29.5	+151	83.8	188	Walk (10.5), Train (21.8)	
	Car P.	16.4	9.7	+52	44.0	94	Walk (24.4), Bus (25.2)	
	Walk	15.3	19.2	-30	25.5	81	Car P. (11.8), Bus (25.2)	0.65
	Bus	14.3	18.0	-29	30.7	68	Walk (33.3), Car P. (9.0)	
	Train	0.3	15.6	-119	1.7	0		
SOUTHAMPTON	Car D.	36.2	24.5	+52	72.5	82	Bus (14.3), Train (26.7)	
	Car P.	15.7	6.3	+42	75.0	49	Bus (31.4), Train (21.4)	
	Walk	7.4	13.0	-25	17.2	23	Car D. (12.1), Bus (39.4)	0.66
	Bus	20.4	25.4	-22	41.6	44	Walk (24.2), Train (9.9)	
	Train	12.4	24.5	-54	28.4	24	Train (16.4), Walk (16.4)	

Continued ....

131

Table 6.5 (continued)

Survey town	Travel mode	Travel mode changes					Principal previous modes	C^1
		A*	B	C	D	E^2		
LIVERPOOL	Car D.	33.5	25.9	+15	64.7	33	Walk (13.6), Bus (22.7)	0.75
	Car P.	16.8	7.6	+18	53.3	25	Car D. (9.1), Bus (48.5)	
	Walk	7.1	9.6	- 5	5.3	13	Car D. (14.3), Bus (64.3)	
	Bus	25.9	41.1	-30	46.9	13	Car D. (5.9), Walk (7.8)	
	Train	14.7	11.7	+ 6	56.5	16	Car D. (31.0), Bus (10.3)	

*   A = Use for Present Trip

    B = Use for Previous Trip

    C = Absolute Change

    D = Same Mode for Pres. and Prev. Trip. (%)

    E = 'Redistributed' Trips

Notes:

1. Contingency coefficient
2. Total present trips - prev/pres trips by same mode
3. Column totals will not sum to 100 because 'Other' modes are excluded.

Source: Office Survey, 1976.

details are provided in Table 6.5. It should be noted that both the Figure and the Table only refer to data for office staff previously in employment; office workers who did not previously have a job are excluded since they only represent additional journeys to work rather than changes.

Columns A and B in Table 6.5 provide a broad comparison of the present and previous modal distributions of work trips, irrespective of destination. Apart from the general similarity between the present modal distribution for each centre (Column A), one of the most interesting features is that the proportion of work trips by bus at Reading, contrary to trends already documented earlier, is higher for the present journey to work than it was before. The remaining changes are more in accord with expectation; there has been a sharp reduction in the share of work journeys by train, an increase in car driver journeys, a moderate increase in the proportion of car passenger trips and a stable or slightly lower share of trips made on foot. These differences mean little however unless they are converted to absolute figures (Column C, Table 6.5) whereupon it emerges that the increase in journeys to work by bus amounts to just 47 extra trips in Reading compared with an additional 192 and 151 car driver journeys respectively. But the reduction in the number of bus journeys in the other centres is not particularly large either, ranging from 22 in Southampton to 30 in Liverpool. It could be argued that bus trips are holding their own but, after allowing for sampling error, it is clear that they are only just managing to do so.

By far the largest absolute reductions in travel mode use for any category occur for journeys to work by train; the absolute change amounts to a loss of 452 trips with a negligible gain of 6 at Liverpool which has a suburban rail network unrivalled by the other four centres. Column D in Table 6.5 therefore shows that former train users are amongst the least likely to continue using the same mode at decentralized locations. The other two more volatile groups of office workers are car passengers and those who previously walked to work. The low figures for the latter suggest that the ability to walk to the office is not an asset which is actively sought when employees change workplaces while the low proportion of "stayers" amongst car passengers reflect the dependence of these employees on others and such arrangements will often change or become impractical if trip destinations or origins no longer coincide. Between 40 and 50 percent of previous bus users continue to use the same mode and they comprise an intermediate group separated from car drivers the majority of whom are likely to continue

using this mode if they already used it before changing
their place of employment. The tendency to continue
using public transport facilities is least well represented in Swindon which has the most dispersed pattern
of office development.

Absolute changes in the use of individual travel
modes disguise the volume of actual inter-modal transfer
which is the total number of present journeys by
mode X minus the total number of previous or present
(whichever is the larger) trips by mode X (Column
E, Table 6.5). These can be classified as 'redistributed'
trips so that some car drivers, for example, will
transfer to train journeys as well as vice versa.
By far the largest number of redistributed trips involve
movements from other modes to car driver journeys
(Column E and Fig. 6.5). Approximately 50 per cent
of all the trips in the sample have been redistributed
(1,634) and 42 percent of these have been transfers
from other modes to car driver trips; bus trips (18
percent) and journeys to work by train (14 percent)
make up a large part of the balance. The principal
sources of trips redistributed to each modal group
are shown in Table 6.5 as the 'principal previous
modes'. In every centre except Liverpool, office
employees who previously travelled to work by bus
or train, especially the latter, are the main source
of additional car driver journeys; at Liverpool several
employees who had previously walked to work are amongst
the principal transfers mainly because central London
staff form such a small proportion of the sample.
Former car drivers who elect to use alternative modes
are far fewer and any redistribution which does take
place is most likely to involve journeys to work on
foot or by train. The majority of transfers to buses
are not car drivers or passengers but employees previously
travelling to work on foot or train users, although
Liverpool is again the exception to this rule. Finally,
the C values (Table 6.5) show a strong association
between previous and present travel mode for the journey
to work, especially in Watford, Liverpool and Southampton.
In Reading and Swindon there is a larger number of
redistributed trips, thus lowering the level of continuing
use of the same mode. There is probably rather less
scope, therefore, for confident prediction of travel
mode choice on the basis of previous modes combined
with the information about the most likely directions
of transfer revealed by the data in Table 6.5.

TRAVEL MODE AND FLEXIBLE HOURS

The distinction between travel mode choices by employees
who are working flexible hours and those who are not
is far from clear (Table 6.6.). Although Reading

Table 6.6

Travel mode choice by office workers on flexible working hours in survey towns

Travel mode	Survey towns									
	Watford		Reading		Swindon		Southampton		Liverpool	
	F^2	NF	F	NF	F	NF	F	NF	F	NF
Car driver	58.3	43.2	37.1	44.2	26.9	49.4	24.8	40.2	37.9	26.2
Car pass.	15.0	9.7	8.7	11.1	22.7	16.8	25.7	11.4	22.7	17.2
Walk	10.0	15.1	7.0	12.6	18.8	17.0	7.1	6.7	7.6	6.9
Bus	6.7	16.5	22.8	22.1	28.6	9.6	31.0	19.6	30.3	30.9
Train	5.0	12.0	20.6	7.9	–	–	7.1	12.7	0.0	15.4
Other	5.0	3.5	3.8	2.1	2.9	6.9	4.3	9.5	1.5	3.4
Absolute total	60	424	1173	195	308	769	210	406	66	233
C^1	0.19		0.15		0.31		0.28		0.48	

Notes: 1.   Contingency coefficient

2.   Employees on flexible hours.

Source: Office Survey, 1976

135

has the largest share of office staff on flexible hours the contingency coefficient is lower than anywhere else perhaps because the imbalance in the contingency table compared with the more balanced samples in the other centres. Hence the value of C at Liverpool (0.48), Southampton (0.28) and Swindon (0.31) indicate that flexible hours may exert some influence on modal choice. However, the character of the relationship in each centre is different; in Southampton 25 percent of the office workers on flexible hours travel to work as car drivers as against 40 percent of the non-flexible respondents, for Liverpool the position is reversed to 38 percent and 26 percent respectively. The Swindon modal distribution is similar to that for Southampton. Likewise, bus trips account for 31 percent of the journeys to work by employees on flexible hours in Southampton compared with 20 percent for other colleagues; in Liverpool the proportion of trips by bus is almost identical while there are no journeys to work by train by 'flexible' staff and 15 percent by non-flexible workers. If the data for Southampton is aggregated on a private/public transport basis then the differences are minor when compared with Liverpool where 68 percent of 'flexible' employees travel to work by private transport compared with 50 percent of the remaining office workers. A higher level of private transport utilization by employees on flexible hours is to be expected and, apart from Liverpool, there is also some evidence for this characteristic at Watford. But this assumption is destroyed at Swindon where 50 percent of the 'flexible' office staff travel to work as car drivers or passengers while the equivalent figure for non-flexible colleagues is 66 percent. The occupational structure of the office labour force has a part to play in the explanation.

Part-time office workers, particularly in Liverpool, have been shown to travel shorter distances and to spend less time travelling to work than full-time office staff (Table 5.6) and this should be reflected in travel mode choice (Table 6.7). In practice, there are only minor differences at Watford but for the Liverpool offices bus trips and journeys on foot are much more important for part-time staff compared with both the overall modal split for the five study towns and full-time office staff in Liverpool. One in five of the part-time staff walk to work and a further 50 percent travel short distances by bus. On the limited evidence from the larger Watford sample, however, it cannot be concluded with any confidence that office centres with a large proportion of part-time workers will generate patterns of mode choice which are significantly different from those of full-time office staff.

Table 6.7

Travel modes for full-time and part-time office staff – Watford and Liverpool

| Travel mode | Survey town | | | | Overall travel mode Distributions (all towns) |
| | Watford | | Liverpool | | |
	Full-time	Part-time	Full-time	Part-time	
Car driver	46.2	39.5	29.7	14.3	38.5
Car pass.	9.4	13.6	18.1	19.0	11.0
Walk	14.8	12.3	6.2	19.0	8.3
Bus	15.1	16.0	29.7	47.6	21.8
Train	10.2	17.3	13.0	–	16.4
Other	4.4	1.2	3.3	–	4.1
Absolute total	392 (100)	81 (100)	276 (100)	21 (100)	3825 (100)

Source: Office Survey 1976

137

CAR SHARING

One of the most interesting characteristics of the journey to work in 1976 compared with 1969 is the degree to which office workers utilize car sharing as a way of reducing the daily costs of commuting. Almost 37 percent of all the trips recorded in the Follow-Up Survey were made in this way, thus helping to reduce the number of vehicles converging on office buildings as well as the demand for any overspill parking in adjacent public car parks or residential streets. It was noted in the Follow-Up Survey that car sharing tends to increase as the distance of office establishments from London increases and this characteristic is repeated in the results for the survey towns (Table 6.8).[8] With four of the towns within or just outside the South East car sharing as a proportion of all trips is, however, lower with 31 percent of the total in this category. In addition some 62 percent (2,292/3,688) of the respondents who travelled to work by car/van on the day of survey in the Follow-Up Survey shared a vehicle with somebody else but the proportion in the survey towns is much lower at 47 percent (1,066/ 2,282). The larger proportion of managers in the survey town offices probably accounts for part at least of the difference between the two surveys.

The sex structure of the office labour force seems to be an important consideration in car sharing, a feature which was not revealed in the analysis based on the Follow-Up offices. While the ratio of car sharing to non-car sharing employees increases from Watford outwards there is also a marked dichotomy between males and females. In all centres the female ratio exceeds 1.0 rising to almost 3 female car sharing trips for every one female travelling independently at Southampton and Liverpool. The ratio for males is always less than 1.0 reaching a maximum of 0.81 in Southampton. Hence, at least twice as many female office workers will travel to work by car/van as do not while the reverse occurs for male office workers. The balance of males/females is therefore crucial since it has been shown earlier that the former are more likely to use private transport; the larger the proportion of females in an office the lower the overall level of private transport trips but their impact on local travel conditions is further reduced by the fact that more of these journeys will involve sharing a vehicle with somebody else. Values of C between 0.27 and 0.36 indicate a moderate association between sex of respondents and incidence of car sharing.

While the probability that car sharing will comprise an important element in work trip behaviour is increased

Table 6.8

Incidence of car/van sharing for the journey to work — by sex

Survey town	Sex	Car sharing by car/van drivers or passengers on day of survey					Not applicable – Respondents walked or used public transport		C[1]	Total trips
		Yes (a)		No (b)		Ratio a/b				
		No.	%	No.	%		No.	%		
Watford	Males	40	21.5	118	63.4	0.34	28	15.1	0.36	186
	Females	81	46.0	49	27.8	1.65	46	26.1		176
Reading	Males	176	24.8	368	51.9	0.48	165	23.3	0.32	709
	Females	136	29.6	84	18.3	1.62	240	52.1		460
Swindon	Males	128	29.6	230	53.2	0.56	66	15.3	0.31	424
	Females	213	35.1	154	24.9	1.38	257	39.9		624
Southampton	Males	89	29.4	110	36.3	0.81	104	34.3	0.27	303
	Females	116	37.7	39	12.7	2.97	153	49.7		308
Liverpool	Males	32	27.1	43	36.4	0.74	43	36.4	0.30	118
	Females	56	33.7	21	12.7	2.67	89	53.6		166
Totals	Males	464	26.7	869	49.9	0.53	406	23.3	–	1740
	Females	602	34.7	347	20.0	1.73	785	45.3		1734
Follow-Up Survey	All respondents	2292	36.5	1396	22.2	1.65	2591	41.3	–	6279

Note: 1. Contingency coefficient.

Sources: Office Survey, 1976
          Follow-Up Survey, 1976

Table 6.9

Incidence of car/van sharing with colleagues working at same office – by sex

Survey town	Sex	Total car sharing	No. sharing with colleagues[1]	% of total	Average vehicle occupancy[2]	Vehicle rotation (%) Yes
Watford	Males	40	20	50.0	2.95 (1.30)[3]	34.4 (12)[4]
	Females	81	28	34.6	3.57 (2.96)	5.8 (4)
Reading	Males	176	96	54.5	3.00 (1.41)	29.3 (46)
	Females	136	49	36.0	3.67 (2.69)	10.5 (13)
Swindon	Males	129	84	65.1	3.01 (0.80)	25.8 (31)
	Females	207	109	52.7	3.60 (1.48)	5.6 (11)
Southampton	Males	89	47	52.8	2.38 (1.31)	23.2 (19)
	Females	116	42	36.2	2.92 (4.42)	6.5 (6)
Liverpool	Males	32	15	50.0	2.44 (1.50)	13.3 (4)
	Females	56	18	32.1	4.44 (3.50)	2.0 (1)
Totals	Males	466	263	56.4 47.9	2.75 (1.26) 3.19(2.13)	
	Females	596	246	41.3	3.64 (3.01)	
Follow-Up Survey	All Respondents	2292	1504	65.6	2.77 (1.40)	

Notes:

1. These figures slightly understate the degree of sharing with colleagues since a small number of respondents failed to answer this part of the question.

2. Respondents were asked to indicate how many colleagues they shared with, including themselves. Average vehicles occupancy is, therefore, total persons, including drivers, divided by number of respondents sharing with colleagues.

3. Based on number of others shared with who were travelling to locations other than the decentralized office.

4. Value in brackets is absolute number of respondents who rotate vehicles involved in car sharing.

by the share of female office staff in each centre,
its actual contribution to a reduction in the number
of vehicles convering an individual buildings or groups
of office buildings in town centres is dependent on
the extent to which sharing involves colleagues at
the same office or individuals travelling to other
workplaces elsewhere in the CBD or somewhere else
in the town or city. The relevant statistics for
sharing with colleagues working at the same office
are given in Table 6.9. The overall level of car/van
sharing with colleagues is lower (48 percent) than
encountered in the Follow-Up Survey (66 percent) but
it seems that this is not attributable to any regional
bias in the location of the survey centres. There
is a very consistent contrast between males and females
which shows that 50-55 percent of males will share
with colleagues but only 32-38 percent of females.
Many of the latter are young office staff who are
conveyed to work by parents or husbands who have destinations elsewhere so that although females are more
likely to share vehicles for the journey to work,
in terms of vehicle generation in the vicinity of
buildings or to city centres they appear to reduce
demand by one-third rather than by one-half or more
for males.

At the same time, however, the average vehicle occupancy
for females sharing with colleagues is higher in all
five centres (2.94-4.44) than for males (2.38-3.01)
which means that the actual reduction in vehicle trips
can be marginally higher for car sharing by female
office staff. There is a much smaller chance that
sharing with workers travelling to some other destination
is important for males compared with females (see
Table 6.9) and car sharing of this kind is only half
as important as sharing with colleagues. Table 6.9
also shows that females tend to be dependent participators
in vehicle sharing since a much smaller proportion
than males rotate the responsibility for providing
cars/vans.

WAITING TIMES AND THE JOURNEY TO WORK

One of the advantages of car sharing is that it provides
an opportunity for office workers to reduce the uncertainty
involved in making the journey to work. This can
be measured by examining the proportion of total journey
times assigned to waiting for transport to arrive
(Table 6.10). The results must be interpreted cautiously
because non-response to the car-sharing section of
the questionnaire was particularly high in Watford
and Reading and the responses may therefore be biased.
It is clear, however, that the majority of car sharing
office workers do not incur any waiting time but of

Table 6.10

Car/van sharing and waiting time for the journey to work

Survey town and method of travel	No. of Trips	No Wait (%)	Waiting time (%)				Non-response[2]
			1-5	6-10	11-15	>16	
WATFORD							
Employees sharing cars/van[1]	122	91.0	0.8	2.5	1.6	4.1	118
Employees not sharing cars/vans	169	87.6	1.8	3.6	1.8	5.4	
Users of other modes	76	72.4	1.3	6.6	3.9	15.7	
READING							
Employees sharing cars/vans	313	84.3	1.3	5.1	3.2	6.0	198
Employees not sharing cars/vans	453	82.8	2.4	6.6	2.6	5.5	
Users of other modes	407	34.6	6.1	17.2	15.5	26.6	
SWINDON							
Employees sharing cars/vans	345	89.6	1.4	1.4	1.2	6.3	27
Employees not sharing cars/vans	385	93.0	0.3	1.6	1.3	3.9	
Users of other modes	325	62.8	1.8	7.4	8.6	19.4	
SOUTHAMPTON							
Employees sharing cars/vans	207	84.1	0.5	1.9	5.8	7.7	3
Employees not sharing cars/vans	152	86.2	3.3	3.9	2.0	4.6	
Users of other modes	261	33.0	6.1	14.9	18.0	27.0	
LIVERPOOL							
Employees sharing cars/vans	88	88.6	1.1	4.5	1.1	4.6	15
Employees not sharing cars/vans	64	87.5	-	4.7	6.2	1.6	
Users of other modes	132	29.5	6.1	8.3	14.4	41.6	

Notes: 1. Employees who travelled to work by car/van on the day of survey but who did not participate in car sharing.

2. Non-response to the car sharing question was high in some centres and the figures are therefore reported.

Source: Office Survey, 1976.

Table 6.11

Waiting time as a proportion of total journey time for public transport work trips to offices in survey towns

Survey town	Mode	No. of trips	No Wait (%)	Waiting time (%)[2] 1-5	6-10	11-15	>16	C[1]
Watford	Bus	74	9.5	2.7	2.7	17.6	60.8	
	Train	54	5.6	9.3	29.6	18.5	37.0	0.67
Reading	Bus	311	19.6	8.0	19.0	18.3	35.0	
	Train	259	11.6	10.4	30.5	15.8	31.7	0.63
Swindon	Bus	162	16.0	4.3	15.4	20.4	43.8	
	Train	2	-	-	50.0	-	50.0	0.61
Southampton	Bus	146	18.5	6.8	15.1	22.6	37.0	
	Train	68	13.2	8.8	23.5	26.5	28.0	0.63
Liverpool	Bus	92	17.4	1.1	8.7	14.1	58.7	
	Train	36	19.4	19.4	25.0	13.9	22.3	0.65

Notes:

1. The contingency coefficient is based on a table in which all modes is cross tabulated with the proportion of waiting time.

2. Number of minutes decribed by respondents as 'wait' as a proportion of total journey time.

Source: Office Survey, 1976.

those who do, rather more can expect to devote more than 16 percent of total journey time to waiting than colleagues who drive directly to the office.[9] Users of public transport are much more likely to incur a period of waiting time although over 60 percent of the Watford and Swindon respondents did not include an allowance for this part of their work journeys. For reasons discussed in the Technical Report it is likely that the rather lower proportions (around 30 percent) for the other three centres are much more realistic but may still understate the necessity to spend at least some time waiting for public transport.[10]

It is therefore to be expected that travel mode and waiting times are closely associated and the values of C are in the range 0.61 - 0.67 (Table 6.11). Most waiting time is incurred by bus and train users in the way clearly illustrated in the table. Less than one in five can expect not to wait while the uncertainty of using buses is clearly higher than it is for trains, particularly in Watford and Liverpool where 59-60 percent of bus users were required to wait at bus stops or interchange points for more than 16 percent of total journey time. It is therefore not surprising that overall mean journey times for journeys to work by bus in all centres are higher than the mean journey times for car drivers. The modal waiting time for train users is 6-10 percent of total time, an advantage which is not inconsiderable for the large number of trips using this mode at Reading.

The scope for incurring waiting time is increased if the journey to work includes several separate stages and although some respondents omitted to record all stages of their journeys an indication of the relationship between number of stages and other variables is provided in Table 6.12. The majority (more than 90 percent) of trips involve up to four stages, whether completed by males or females, although because the latter tend to use public transport it is more likely that their journeys to work will be broken up into at least three stages. But the sex of respondents is not a good indicator of the complexity of work trips, especially in Southampton (0.16) and Swindon (0.21). Occupation status is also only moderately associated with this variable. Much more important are travel mode and trip time which to some extent are interdependent variables. The values of C are highest in relation to travel mode with a peak of 0.81 in Watford, decreasing at centres further from London to 0.69. Those centres with decentralized patterns of office development (Liverpool and Swindon) do not have the highest values of C even though it might be expected that public transport trips would be less direct in these instances than in centres with highly centralized office location

144

Table 6.12
Relationship between number of stages in the journey
to work and selected trip characteristics

Trip characteristic	Survey towns				
	Watford C^1	Reading C	Swindon C	Southampton C	Liverpool C
Travel mode	0.81	0.72	0.72	0.69	0.69
Trip time	0.64	0.59	0.62	0.68	0.52
Trip distance	0.53	0.49	0.51	0.29	0.40
Occupation status	0.32	0.27	0.26	0.29	0.36
Sex	0.29	0.23	0.21	0.16	0.27
N =	477	1365	1077	613	299

Note: 1. Contingency coefficient. H_0 = No difference in number of stages in the journey to work with respect to travel mode, trip time, trip distance and occupation status respectively.

Source: Office Survey, 1976

patterns such as Watford or Reading. The values of
C for trip time are rather lower, between 0.52 and
0.68 but in general the more time consuming a work
journey is the more likely it is that it will comprise
more than two or three stages. The relationship with
trip distance is rather weaker for all the centres
and this confirms the importance of travel mode since
many longer distance trips are made by car with the
result that multi-stage journeys to work are much
less likely.

JOURNEY TO WORK ARRIVAL TIMES

The combined effect of travel mode and car sharing
on the spread of employee arrival times at the offices
in the sample was not found to create any notable
differences at the case study offices used in the
Follow-Up Survey.[11] The situation is much the same
in the study towns when travel mode for the journey
to work and arrival times are compared (Fig. 6.6).
In Swindon the majority of car drivers tend to arrive
later than other groups, a situation which also occurs
in Liverpool but the general pattern is one of coincidence
between curves rather than of prominent differences.
There is some evidence, however, that arrival times
are different for car/van drivers who participate
in car sharing and those who do not. The heavy lines
on Fig. 6.7, with the exception of Reading, are all
to the left of the lighter lines which represent employees
who travel independently by car/van. Thus, at Watford
for example, 45 percent of car-sharing staff arrived
before 08.30 hours compared with 28 percent of the
remaining car/van trips; the equivalent differences
for Swindon, Southampton and Liverpool are 55/48 percent,
63/49 percent and 66/65 percent respectively. Apart
from Reading, therefore, there is clear evidence that
car sharing not only reduces the number of vehicles
used for the journey to work but also spreads the
demand for peak hour travel. There is of course an
occupational effect to consider here since car sharing
is more prominent among clerical and related workers
who are more likely to be required to start work earlier
than (or at fixed times) some other categories of
office staff. They are also more likely to be part
of a flexible hours programme and, therefore, have
an opportunity to reduce journey to work delays by
travelling outside the peak period. With values of
C between 0.22 and 0.28 it can only be concluded,
however, that there is a low/moderate association
between car sharing and arrival times at decentralized
offices in all five towns.

The case study data used in the Follow-Up Survey
also showed that trip time for the journey to work

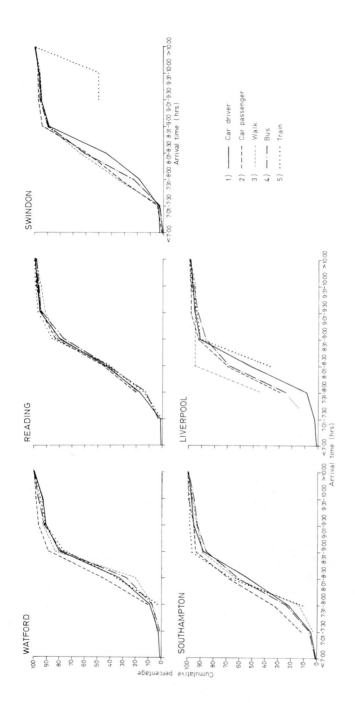

Figure 6.6 Travel mode and arrival times at offices in survey towns.

147

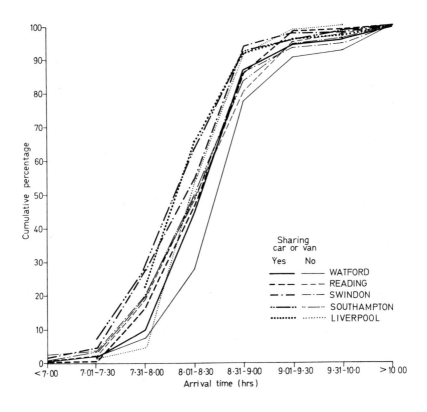

Figure 6.7   Car sharing and arrival times at office in
survey towns.

Table 6.13

Relationship between travel mode, occupation status, trip time, trip distance, and whether office staff are on flexible hours and arrival times at offices in survey towns

Selected variables	Survey towns				
	Watford C^1	Reading C	Swindon C	Southampton C	Liverpool C
Flexible hours	0.08	0.30*	0.44*	0.34*	0.45*
Travel mode	0.27	0.30*	0.32*	0.32*	0.47*
Occupation Status	0.41*	0.20*	0.34*	0.28*	0.39*
Trip time	0.40*	0.34*	0.41*	0.54*	0.54*
Trip distance	0.36*	0.14	0.26*	0.24	0.31

Note: 1. Contingency coefficient. The asterisks denote the associated values of X^2 which are significant at the 0.05 level, H_o = No relationship between the selected variables with reference to arrival times at decentralized offices.

appeared to affect arrival times more than any other
variable with employees having trips of less than
35 minutes duration more likely to arrive before colleagues with higher journey times.[12]   This is also
the case for the offices in the five study centres
where values of C, particularly at Swindon, Southampton
and Liverpool, indicate a strong association between
these variables which has a similar direction to that
noted for the case study establishments (Table 6.3).
In common with the earlier results, trip distance
is a less reliable indicator except at Watford (0.36)
where there is a moderate association.   Only two of
the contingency tables upon which the C values are
based have X^2 values which permit rejection of the
null hypothesis given in Table 6.13, while all the
X^2 values for trip times are significant.   Occupation
status is also associated with arrival times to a
significant degree but the strength of the relationship
is lower than for trip times.

OFFICE LOCATION AND TRAVEL MODE DISTRIBUTION

The analysis so far has clearly demonstrated that
the configuration of office development within each
urban area does seem to exert some influence on the
modal split of the trips generated by office establishments.   The differences are most clearly exemplified
by, on the one hand, Swindon with its very decentralized
location pattern and, on the other hand, Watford or
Reading with their more highly centralized distribution
of offices.   There remains, however, a need to consider
further whether the aggregate differences in the modal
split between the five centres conceal variations
at individual office establishments which result from
the availability of public transport or variables
such as the sex ratio, the managerial and professional/
technical and clerical ratio or the ratio of central
London to all other recruits at individual offices
in the sample.   In order to explore these possibilities
some of the journey to work and related information
for selected offices in each centre (mainly those
with more than 20 respondents) have been extracted
and listed for comparative purposes in Table 6.14.
The assessment of the level of access of each office
to bus and/or rail services is clearly subjective
but it can be seen that a variety of locations is
represented.

Offices with a very good access to public transport
services are usually characterised by above average
levels of train utilisation rather than use of bus
services for the journey to work.   The latter proportion
is usually in accord with the norm for less well positioned buildings.   Thus, office 90 (Reading), office
82 (Watford), office 98 (Southampton) and office 71

Table 6.14

Selected attributes of individual offices and the modal split for the journey to work

Study town and office No.	Sample	M/F ratio	MP/SC ratio	CL/OR ratio	Access to bus/rail[2]	Modal split (%)					C/V Sharing[1] (%)	≤35 mins (%)	Trips ≤10km
						Car D	Car P	Walk	Bus	Train			
Reading													
(90)	560	3:1	2:1	1.2:1	Very good	40.0	7.7	6.2	16.8	26.2	34.3	69.7	57.3
(93)	210	1.6:1	1:1	1.5:1	Good	54.3	7.1	6.7	13.8	15.7	32.1	68.7	59.8
(84)	409	1:1.3	1:8	1:2.6	Good	24.2	10.8	8.1	35.2	15.6	61.1	65.8	69.9
(64)	48	2.4:1	1:1.1	1:1	Very Good	62.5	10.4	2.1	18.7	6.2	44.1	70.9	56.5
(76)	32	1.1:1	1.1:1	1:16	Limited (Bus)	34.4	15.6	18.7	18.7	6.2	50.0	75.0	87.5
(77)	21	1.3:1	2:1	1:7	Limited (Bus)	47.6	14.3	19.0	19.0	–	33.0	76.2	80.9
Swindon													
(79)	83	1:2.5	1:5.3	1:15	Limited (Bus)	37.3	14.5	33.7	9.6	–	41.3	93.8	90.1
(85)	234	1.4:1	1:1.4	1:1.6	Very Limited (Bus)	62.4	18.8	6.0	9.0	0.9	47.7	87.2	65.6
(89)	108	1:1.1	1:13.5	1:1.9	Very Limited (Bus)	30.5	18.6	31.4	6.8	–	52.1	93.2	89.0
(94)	540	1:2	1:4.5	1:7.4	Limited (Bus)	36.1	19.6	15.7	21.9	–	47.5	90.1	88.5
(92)	65	1:1.4	1:2	1:20	Very Limited (Bus)	53.8	16.9	21.5	6.2	–	44.9	95.3	83.1

Table 6.14 (continued)

Study town and Office No.	Sample	M/F ratio	MP/SC ratio	CL/OR ratio	Access to bus/rail[2]	Modal split (%)					C/V Sharing[1] (%)	<35 mins (%)	Trips <10km
						Car D	Car P	Walk	Bus	Train			
Watford													
(96)	214	1:1.1	1:1.8	1:4.9	Good	47.2	7.9	13.6	16.8	11.2	38.2	63.8	65.8
(80)	151	1:1.6	1:5.0	1:11.3	Good	38.4	11.9	16.6	14.6	14.6	50.0	61.3	60.4
(81)	43	1:1	1:1.3	1:7.6	Good	58.1	16.3	11.6	4.7	2.3	43.8	86.1	72.1
(82)	18	1:1.3	1:1	1:12.0	Good	66.7	–	–	11.1	22.2	10.0	61.2	57.0
Southampton													
(73)	27	1:2.9	1:5.8	0:27.0	Good	25.9	7.4	7.4	37.0	3.7	37.5	74.0	96.3
(65)	111	1:1.4	1:4.2	1:2.0	Good	43.2	13.5	6.3	25.2	4.5	58.5	66.7	81.8
(66)	39	2:9.1	1:1.1	1:3.1	Good	38.5	15.4	–	15.4	23.1	40.7	56.5	44.8
(67)	53	1:7.1	1:2.2	1:5.1	Poor	60.4	22.6	–	3.8	9.4	60.0	80.8	55.8
(98)	63	1:9.1	1:19.3	1:28.5	Very Good	4.8	4.8	17.5	12.7	55.6	47.4	54.0	64.5
(72)	116	1:8.1	1:3.1	1:9.1	Limited (Bus)	50.9	6.0	4.3	24.1	2.6	46.7	64.0	81.4
(47)	172	1:2.4	1:20.3	1:54.6	Good	24.5	27.3	9.3	34.3	4.1	81.9	75.0	87.6

Table 6.14 (continued)

Study town and Office No.	Sample	M/F ratio	MP/SC ratio	CL/OR ratio	Access to bus/rail[2]	Modal split (%) Car D	Car P	Walk	Bus	Train	C/V Sharing[1] (%)	≤35 mins (%)	Trips <10km
Liverpool													
(71)	72	2.4:1	1:1.8	1:4.6	Very Good	26.4	13.9	–	13.9	34.7	44.7	56.9	62.5
(83)	206	1:2.5	1:7.1	1:40.2	Very Good	31.1	20.4	9.2	37.9	1.0	63.6	75.2	80.3

Notes:

1. Proportion of employees who travelled to work by car/van on the day of survey who shared their vehicles with colleagues at the same office and individuals working elsewhere.

2. Very good = town centre location immediately adjacent to bus and rail services.

   Good = primarily dependent on bus services in town centre but rail services within $\frac{1}{4}$ – $\frac{1}{2}$ mile walking distance.

   Limited (bus) = primarily offices in non-town centre locations served by bus routes covering only part of the urban area.

   Very Limited (bus) = offices in outer urban areas served by one or two radial bus routes only.

   Poor = Offices without bus or rail services within $\frac{1}{4}$ – $\frac{1}{2}$ mile walking distance.

Source: Office Survey, 1976.

(Liverpool) all generate significant proportions of rail travel which can undoubtedly be attributed to location (as well as fare concessions at office 71, Southampton). But user levels for bus services are similar to the average for the centre concerned and do not seem to reflect the variety of services available in each case. Yet there are exceptions to this relationship; such as office 64 (Reading) which occupies a building immediately adjacent to the railway station (almost opposite office 90) but train services are only used for the journey to work of some 6 percent of the respondents. This office illustrates the operation of other variables such as the male/female ratio which favours the former and a balanced occupation ratio which, together with the residential distribution of employees, encourages journeys to work by car rather than train or bus. Offices with good access to public transport such as 84 and 93 (Reading), 96 or 80 (Watford), or 65, 66 or 47 (Southampton) all have above average use of both bus and train services for work journeys which in the case of the latter is a by-product of the extra walking distance from stations and the possibility of having to transfer to another mode of transport to reach the offices. Therefore the proportion of train users at office 93 or office 84 is lower than at office 90, or bus services are better used (such as offices 65 and 66 in Southampton). Again, however, it is worth noting that an additional factor, in at least some of these cases, is that at offices with a high male/female ratio journeys to work by train comprise a larger proportion of all journeys and vice-versa for bus journeys to offices with a low or adverse male/female ratio. The occupation ratio, which in part reflects the sex ratio, also seems to affect the bus/rail balance at locations where a reasonable opportunity exists to make a choice between these two modes.

The effect of limited or very limited public transport services (bus only) on modal split appears to depend on the pattern of office development. All the offices in Swindon are widely dispersed and have limited public transport services with the result that journeys to work on foot are far more important at all the offices, except office 85 which has a low male/female and occupation ratio, than in any of the other centres. Public transport hardly provides for any work journeys except at office 94 which has a high male/female and occupation ratio, but because of the close juxtaposition of residential areas and employment centres there has not been a reciprocal demand for car-based journeys to work. The data from office 85 again contradicts this generalisation but with 1.4 males for every female office worker and one central London recruit for every 1.6 recruits from other sources the circumstances clearly favour journeys to work by private car to a degree which overrides the more general effect of the location of the office within Swindon on work travel. A similar effect can be observed in Reading where offices some distance from the town centre such as 76 and 77 also attract a larger than expected proportion of walking trips even though male and managerial/ professional staff comprise large proportions of the respondents in each office. Where poor or limited public transport access coincides with a centralized pattern of office location such as offices 72 or 67 in Southampton the ability to substitute public or car driver/passenger trips with the walking mode is clearly limited and in these cirumstances employers must either provide their own services or negotiate special facilities with local bus companies (office 72) or, alternatively, office staff must rely more on car sharing and both these offices have values for these variables which are towards the top end of the range shown in Table 6.14. Occupation and sex structure effects are again operational, however, because at office 83 (Liverpool) which has a limited bus service the scope for substituting with private transport is limited because of the high ratio of technical/clerical to other staff and therefore the lower levels of car ownership mentioned earlier in this chapter. A similar situation is found to occur at office 47 in Southampton.

NOTES AND REFERENCES

(1) Household car ownerhip (%) for the resident population of each study town in 1971 was as follows: (No Car, One Car, Two Cars):

Watford	44.1,	45.6,	10.3
Reading	51.2,	41.6,	7.2
Swindon	51.3,	42.7,	6.0
Southampton	50.9,	42.4,	7.6
Liverpool	67.3,	28.5,	4.2

Source: Office of Population Censuses and Surveys, Census 1971, England and Wales, Availability of Cars, H.M.S.O., London 1973.

(2) P.W. Daniels, 'Transport changes generated by decentralized offices', Regional Studies, Vol. 6, 1972, pp. 273-89. A further paper entitled 'Transport changes generated by decentralized offices: a second survey' is currently being considered for publication in Regional Studies.

(3) Means of transport (%) for total persons working
     in each area in 1971 was as follows (Car, on
     foot, bus, train, other):

Watford	44.1,	19.9,	17.9,	7.9,	10.2
Reading	39.3,	17.7,	27.1,	3.9,	12.0
Swindon	39.3,	21.7,	20.0,	0.4,	18.6
Southampton	43.4,	13.9,	27.3,	1.8,	13.6
Liverpool	27.8,	14.1,	43.3,	7.5,	7.3

     Source: Office of Population Censuses and
             Surveys Census 1971, England and Wales,
             Workplace and Transport to Work Tables,
             Part II (10% sample), H.M.S.O., London
             1975.

(4) P.W. Daniels, 'Vehicle sharing for the journey
     to work by office employees', recently submitted
     to Transportation Research, 1979.

(5) The bar graphs have been subdivided to show the
     share of the total trips represented which
     are undertaken by each of the major groups
     of recruits.

(6) This is also estimated in the Follow-Up Survey,
     see P.W. Daniels, A Follow-Up Study of the
     Journey to Work at Decentralized Offices in
     Britain : Final Report (Part I), Departments
     of Environment and Transport, London 1978,
     section 4.

(7) See note (1).

(8) P.W. Daniels, op. cit., 1978 (Part I), Table
     4.19.

(9) It may appear that this group does not incur
     any waiting time at all but the method of coding
     used assigns modal category to the principal
     part of a trip which may involve short stages
     using other means of transport.

(10) See A.W. Duffett and P.W. Daniels, The Journey
     to Work at Decentralized Offices in Britain
     - (1) A Follow-Up Study (2) at Groups of Offices
     in Watford, Reading, Swindon, Southampton and
     Liverpool : Final Report (Part IV), Survey
     Design Data Processing and Analysis, Departments
     of Environment and Transport, London 1979.

(11) Also discussed in P.W. Daniels, A Follow-Up Study
of the Journey to Work at Decentralized Offices
in Britain : Final Report Part II, Case Studies
at New Malden, Southampton, Leicester and Durham,
Departments of Environment and Transport, London
1978, paras. 10.8-10.11.

(12) Ibid., Figure 10.3.

7 Summary and conclusions

This study has provided a good opportunity to see whether the results derived from a survey of travel to work at decentralized offices scattered throughout Britain provides an adequate basis for predicting the journey to work characteristics of office staff in major groups of these offices in specific urban areas. The results suggest that the answer to this question should be positive, but with the important qualification that the detailed location of office buildings within an urban area does seem to exert considerable influence on the trip characteristics of office workers. This factor clearly could not be allowed for in the Follow-Up Survey which was confined to single offices. The principal example of the importance of the location variable in the survey towns is the contrast in trip distances and modal structure of work journeys for office staff in Reading and Swindon.

A further opportunity has also been provided to examine hypotheses III and IV which have been used to guide the research (see Chapter 1). For the Follow-Up Survey it was concluded that there did not appear to be a close relationship between the availability of transport services and the structure of journey to work travel to decentralized offices (hypothesis III). The more concentrated sample used in this report has allowed this conclusion to be examined further.

The pattern of office development does create some differences in the accessibility of offices by public transport but not entirely in the direction anticipated. Although Swindon has a highly dispersed pattern this has not occurred completely at the expense of access by bus services; Southampton has a more centralized pattern but still has more offices which are not served by public transport.

Most of the decentralized offices included in the survey completed their moves after 1970, particularly those moves involving large numbers of staff. It has been found that the retention of central London staff still depends on distance moved by their employers. Liverpool, according to estimates provided by employers, therefore attract the lowest proportion of central London staff. It may be however that housing availability, such as in Swindon, modifies the distance decay effect generally revealed in the mobility of this group of employees. Shortfalls in the supply of office staff are not necessarily made good by recruiting local labour. It seems that many of the larger organisations use decentralization as a 'centralization' exercise which involves bringing together staff from other parts of the country. Therefore the size of a decentralizing organisation, the spatial disposition of other parts of its activities and the status of the decentralized establishment in the organisational hierarchy will determine the final demand for recruits from local sources.

In general there is a close association between estimates made by employers of their recruitment and the actual structure of response to the employee questionnaire survey. Central London recruits are over represented in the Reading sample but under represented elsewhere. Employees in managerial occupations occur with a higher frequency than expected in Watford and Reading, both of which are therefore deficient in clerical workers. Swindon and Southampton have more employees in clerical occupations than expected from the overall distribution of clerical workers in the five study centres. The share of labour demand generated by decentralized offices which is satisfied by local recruits comprises an important lag effect whereby the local supply increases its share some 2-3 years after decentralization when the impetus for attracting central London staff has waned. Employers must then either recruit staff from other parts of the country or must increasingly depend on local sources.

Some 50 percent of the central London recruits who needed to obtain housing as a result of decentralization left accommodation within Greater London and approximately one-third came from Inner London. Conversely, about 70 percent of the recruits from elsewhere relocated from areas outside Greater London. The result is that the residential changes created by decentralization comprises a 'predictable' component of movement over similar distances from contiguous residential areas in and around the origin city. There is also a second, but less predictable, component of residential mobility which is spatially diverse and the result of a more variable set of factors. It has been shown that the critical determinant of the volume of housing demand at reception centres by decentralized office workers is the proportion of central London recruits and recruits from elsewhere, particularly at locations where it is essential for employees to change address in order to be accessible to their offices. For every one migrant office worker who first seeks housing outside the reception centre, two will seek accommodation within the urban area. Occupation status affects the spatial pattern of housing demand but the location of the reception town and the quality of its housing stock can modify the effect of this variable. The annual demand for housing accommodation by decentralized office workers has a clear bi-modal distribution. As expected the first peak occurs shortly after offices have moved but there is a second, and lower, peak some 7-9 years after office moves are completed. This is probably related to recruitment cycles and staff turnover.

These socio-economic and residential mobility attributes of the office workers in the sample help to account for the journey to work patterns in each urban area. But the well established dichotomy between the journey to work times and distances of male and female office staff is clearly confirmed in each of the five centre, especially for the distances travelled to work at the office establishments. A more detailed analysis of male and female journeys shows that there is more variability between the two groups when they are compared across the five centres; rather more than the variability which exists within each centre. Female office workers, however, display more variation in trip characteristics between, as well as within, the urban centres than their male counterparts. It is suggested that this arises from the greater dependence of female office staff on others for transport to work and also reflects the different patterns of office development in the five towns.

Trip characteristics related to occupation status and previous workplace of office workers conform to the results of the Follow-Up Survey. Almost all the local recruits travel less than 10km to work with most of the long distance trips in excess of 22 km undertaken by recruits from elsewhere (Reading and Swindon) or by central London recruits. For individual journeys to work the principal determinant of trip time is trip distance which may account for up to 45 percent of the variation in trip time. The method of travel used explains a further 10 percent in Reading, Swindon and Southampton but is displaced by car sharing for the Watford and Liverpool samples. The distances travelled to work by individual office workers are more difficult to predict by reference to a small number of independent variables and the proportion of the variation explained is lower. Disaggregated mean trip distances by travel mode for male and female office workers show a tendency towards heterogeneity rather than homogeneity. Most of the variability occurs at Reading and Watford. Mean trip times and travel mode by sex showed more homogeneity with inter- and intra- centre ranges much closer than the equivalent data for journey distances.

Office workers from households with at least one car comprise a major part of the sample; one in four of all the respondents come from households with two or more cars. One- and two-car households are over represented in Reading and Swindon but both groups are under represented in the Liverpool sample. There is a moderate association between car ownership and travel mode choice for the journey to work in all five centres. Between a half and one-third of the journeys to work by bus or on foot are generated by office workers from households which do not own or have access to a car/van. As we have now come to expect the majority of central London recruits drive or travel to work by train at the decentralized locations. Utilisation of local bus services largely depends on the patronage of local recruits and the composition of the office labour force again emerges as a key determinant of the modal structure of journey to work travel to decentralized offices. Occupation status and travel mode choice also show a moderate degree of association.

The majority of journeys to work by car drivers in all the centres are made by male office staff while most car passenger journeys are made by females. Hence, it is suggested that office centres with a high male/female ratio of respondents will generate a higher proportion of car driver trips. There is some support for this hypothesis but other factors such as the detailed location of individual offices or occupation structure modify the relationship.

Contrasting distributions of office premises in the study towns in relation to public transport are reflected in user levels. There are twice as many train journeys by Reading office workers as expected but only a negligible number (2) at Swindon. Public transport in general is used at a higher level in the survey towns than in the Follow-Up Survey. This may indicate that public transport is beginning to regain some of the lost ground but the rate of recovery is very slow.

Travel mode change is not a central issue in this study but a brief reference shows that there has been a sharp reduction in the proportion of work journeys by train, an increase in car driver journeys, a moderate increase in the proportion of car passenger journeys and a stable or slightly lower share of journeys to work made on foot. In the Reading sample the post-decentralization share of bus journeys has increased but in absolute terms the change is much smaller than the absolute increase in car driver or passenger trips.

In common with the Follow-Up Survey results, car sharing is higher in the urban areas furthest from London, but the overall level of car sharing (with four of the towns within 90 miles of London) is lower.

There is a marked dichotomy in car sharing activity
by male and female office staff with twice as many
females travelling as car passengers as those who
do not. The ratio of male/females in the office labour
force is therefore a crucial factor affecting the
level of car sharing. Car sharing not only reduces
the number of private vehicles generated by the offices
in each centre but it has also been shown that it
spreads the demand for peak hour travel.

More detailed reference to the relationship between
office location and the travel mode structure of work
journeys shows that offices with very good access
to public transport services are usually characterised
by above average levels of train rather than bus utilisation. The male/female ratio and the occupation
ratio also affects the private/public transport balance
irrespective of whether both, or only one, of the
principal public transport modes are easily accessible.
In cases where public transport services are limited
the effect of modal structure depends on the pattern
of office development. The dispersed pattern in Swindon
results in a large proportion of journeys on foot
and less dependence on public transport when compared
with the centralized pattern of offices in Reading
or, to a lesser extent, Southampton.

APPENDIX

DEPARTMENT OF GEOGRAPHY

UNIVERSITY OF LIVERPOOL
ROXBY BUILDING, P.O. BOX 147, LIVERPOOL L69 3BX

OFFICE DECENTRALIZATION PROJECT

Telephone: 051-709 6022 (Ext 2729)

OFFICE DISPERSAL JOURNEY TO WORK SURVEY

Dear Sir/Madam,

I have been asked by the Department of the Environment to conduct a follow-up survey which examines the effects of office dispersal from central London.

I am particularly interested in your present journey to work, especially the time you take and the methods of travel you use.

Journeys to work should be as short and direct as possible. Transport authorities can only help to achieve this if the character of these movements can be identified.

This study is an attempt to do this and, therefore, I would be most grateful for your help.

The answers you provide on this questionnaire will be treated as strictly confidential.

Yours faithfully,

P.W.Daniels

Dr. P.W. Daniels,
Director,
Office Decentralization Project

PLEASE READ EVERY QUESTION AND TICK APPROPRIATE BOX OR WRITE AS REQUIRED ☑

RESIDENCE

1. Before taking up your first job at <u>this office</u> where was your permanent address?
   By 'this office' we mean with this employer in this building or group of buildings.

   Street (exclude house no.) ....

   Village or locality ....

   Town or postal district ....

2. Are you still living at the address given in question 1?   Yes ☐

   No ☐

   If <u>YES</u>, please go to Question 4.

3. If <u>NO</u>, please list in order, starting with your <u>present address</u> and working back to the address given in question 1, all the addresses which you have since occupied.
   Include the month and year when you first moved to each one.

	Street (exclude house no.)	Village or locality	Town or postal district	Month	Year
1					
2					
3					
4					
5					
6					
7					
8					

4. What was your permanent address on 31st December, 1969?

   Street (exclude house no.) ....

   Village or locality ....

   Town or postal district ....

OCCUPATION

1. (a) What is the full title of your <u>present job</u> at this office?

   ....

   (b) What was the full title of the <u>job you previously held</u> immediately before coming to work at this office?

   ....

2. It is not always clear from your job title what sort of work you do. Therefore could you describe your work in the space below.

   (a) <u>present job</u>

   ....

   ....

   (b) <u>job you previously held</u>

   ....

   ....

1. What time did you leave home for work this morning?

    e.g. 7.25, 8.38, 9.16 etc. ....

2. Could you please indicate, as shown in the example, how you travelled to work, and how many minutes you spent on each part of your journey:

    (a) this morning

    (b) in the job previously held

    (i)   *Do not forget the walking part of your journey, e.g. from home to bus stop; from car park to office.*

    (ii) *Could you also include the waiting parts of your journey, e.g. at the bus stop, at the station.*

    (iii) *If you travel to work as a car/van passenger, please write* car passenger *for the appropriate part of your journey and give the journey time.*

    (iv) *For (b) give the usual journey and average times.*

this is an example		(a) present job		(b) job previously held	
leave home					
Walk	2				
Car	5				
Wait for train	5				
Train	7				
Walk	2				
Wait for Bus	3				
Bus	8				
Walk	3				
arrive work					

This section includes vehicles such as cars, vans, three-wheelers, motor-cycles etc.

If you were <u>either</u> a passenger <u>or</u> a driver of one of these vehicles this morning:

1. Do you usually share a car/van on your journey to work?

    Yes ☐   *If <u>NO</u>, please go to the*
    car/van availability
    No ☐   *section below.*

2. If <u>YES</u>, does the same person usually provide the vehicle you travel in or is there a rotation of cars/vans?

    Same vehicle ☐

    Rotation of vehicles ☐

3. Do you usually share with other people working at this office?

    Yes ☐

    No ☐

4. How many people, including yourself, usually travel in the car/van?

    .... travelling to work at <u>this office</u>

    .... travelling to work elsewhere

<u>present job</u> | <u>job previously held</u> *immediately before coming to work at this office*

1. (a) Does your household have, or have the full use of, the following?

    No car/van ☐

    One car/van ☐

    Two or more cars/vans ☐

    (b) Did your household have, or have the full use of, the following?

    No car/van ☐

    One car/van ☐

    Two or more cars/vans ☐

2. (a) If 'one car/van', what usually happens to it during your working day?

    Not Used ☐

    Kept at my place of work ☐

    Kept at someone else's place of work ☐

    Other (please specify) ....
    ....

    (b) If 'one car/van', what usually happened to it during your working day?

    Not Used ☐

    Kept at my place of work ☐

    Kept at someone else's place of work ☐

    Other (please specify) ....
    ....

3. (a) Can you drive a car/van?

    Yes ☐

    No ☐

    (b) Could you drive a car/van?

    Yes ☐

    No ☐

168

1. In which month and year did you take up your first job at <u>this office</u>?

   Month .... Year ....

2. Were you working at <u>this office</u> in December 1969?

   Yes ☐
   No ☐

3. If <u>No</u>, were you employed by your present employer in another office building in this town or suburb in December, 1969?

   Yes ☐
   No ☐

4. Immediately before taking up your job at <u>this office</u> where did you work?

   (a) Not previously employed ☐

   (b) For your <u>present</u> employer in:

      (i) the centre of London ☐

      (ii) in this town or suburb ☐

      (iii) in another town or suburb (please state where) ☐

   ....

   ....

   (c) For <u>another</u> employer in:
      (i) the centre of London ☐

      (ii) this town or suburb ☐

      (iii) in another town or suburb ☐

5. <u>For 4c</u>, please state the name and address of the employer.

   Name ....

   Address ....

   ....

6. <u>For 4c</u>, when did you cease working there?

   Month .... Year ....

1. Are you: Male ☐
   Female ☐

2. Are you: Married ☐
   Single ☐
   Widowed ☐
   Other ☐

3. What was your age at your last birthday?

   .... years

4. Are you:

   In <u>full-time</u> employment at this office (over 30 hours per week) ☐

   OR In <u>part-time</u> employment at this office

      (i) over 10 hours per week and up to and including 30 hours ☐

      (ii) 10 hours or less per week ☐

5. Can you remember whether you completed a questionnaire in 1969 which asked you about your journey to work to <u>this office</u>?

   <u>YES</u>, I completed that questionnaire ☐

   <u>I MAY HAVE</u> completed that questionnaire ☐

   <u>NO</u>, I did not complete that questionnaire ☐

------------------------------------ THANK YOU FOR YOUR CO-OPERATION ------------------------------------

1. Would you be willing, if required at a later date, to answer a further questionnaire on a similar subject?

   Yes ☐ No ☐

   *If YES, would you please write your name below and return this slip to your employer. We will **not** see these slips but if necessary we will contact you through your employer using the number on the slip, which matches the number on the front of this questionnaire.*

   Name ....

Index

14, 31; temporal aspects of demand for, 55, 76–80

Insurance offices, 15

Labour force: catchment area, 80, 94; and local public transport, 161; pattern of supply and demand, 45–7, 94, 159; recruitment of, 37–47; structure of, 37–47; Swindon catchment area, 30; Watford catchment area, 12–13; see also staff

Liverpool: car ownership in, 98–100, 114–124; car sharing in, 33, 138–141; car park space in, 35; distance to work in, 83–5, 89, 90, 95, 96, 97; flexible hours in, 100–105; local staff recruitment in, 39, 65; and location of offices in survey, 30; place of recruitment of staff in, 39–45; previous place of residence, 71; public transport in, 33; response rates in, 21, 22; staff mobility in, 65; and time to work, 91, 92, 95, 96–8; and transfer of staff from London, 37–8, 65; waiting time in, 141–6

Location of Offices Bureau, 1, 9, 14, 72

London Transport, 12

Male staff: and car ownership, 114–118; and car sharing, 138–141, 162; distance to work of, 83–5, 88–98, 160; and flexible hours, 47–52; mobility of, 55–61; and mode of travel, 116–118, 124–5, 126–8, 154; occupation status of, 88–98; and part time work, 47–52; previous workplace of, 88–98; recruitment of, 39; time of journey of, 85–7, 88–98, 160

Managerial staff: car ownership amongst, 114; car sharing amongst, 138; choice of area of residence of, 41, 73–75; distance to work of, 88–90; time of journey to work of, 91–8

Manufacturing services, 12, 15

Mobility: of office staff, 55–61; and recruitment policy, 62, 63

Multiple regression analysis, 105–111

Occupational status: and arrival time, 149, 150; and car ownership, 100; and choice of area of residence, 73, 80, 96, 159; and complexity of journey to work, 144, 160; and distance to work, 88–98; and likelihood of moving with employer, 41; and mode of travel, 5, 41, 122–4, 155; in multiple regression analysis, 105–111; time of journey to work, 88–98

Office employment, growth of, 12

Part-time work, 47–52; distance of journey for, 97–8; mode of travel for, 136–7; time of journey for, 97–8, 136–7

Planning policy, 12–14

Professional class: car ownership amongst, 114; choice of area of residence, 73, 75, distance to work of, 88–90; mode of travel of, 122–4, 155; time to work of, 91–8

Professional and scientific services, 15

Public administration, 15

Public transport: accessibility of, 150–155, 158, 162; compared with car in G.L.C., 3; and locally recruited staff, 161; and location of offices, 4, 5, 22, 24–35, 162; service provided by, 2; use of by sex, 116; use of in Survey Towns compared with follow-up survey, 118–119; waiting time for, 144

Rail, railways, see train

Reading: area chosen for residence, 73; car ownership in, 98–100, 114–124; car sharing in, 33, 138–141; car park space in, 34–5; distance to work in, 83–5, 89, 90, 95, 96; flexible hours in, 100–105; labour force catchment area, 64; local staff recruitment, 39, 63; office development policy, 13–14; place of recruitment of staff, 39–45; previous place of residence, 68; response rates, 20–1; staff mobility in, 63; and time to work, 91, 92, 95, 96–8; transfer of staff from London to, 37–8,